Contents

Editorial

Caroline Sweetman

'The way we define citizenship is intimately linked to the kind of society and political community we want.'
(Mouffe 1992a, 25, quoted in Lister 1997, 103)

Citizenship is a famously slippery concept – different people use it in a range of different ways. But a very basic definition is that a citizen is 'a legally recognised national of a state, either native or naturalised' (*New Oxford Dictionary of English*, 1998). Focusing on citizenship means thinking about the relationships between individuals and the states in which they live. Are individual women and men considered as equal citizens? What about people from minority groups, or recent migrants? What difference does having citizenship rights make to people's lives?

On one side of the citizenship 'coin', citizenship equals *entitlement to a range of rights*. To what extent do different states guarantee the civil, political, economic, and social rights of women and men, established in national constitutions or international agreements? How relevant are these rights to particular economic and cultural groupings? Whose rights are not acknowledged or upheld, and why?

On the other side of the citizenship coin is the issue of *participation in governance*. Is the government democratic? Are structures of governance efficient, and responsive to people's needs? (Governance structures are not only national, but run all the way up through society, from village councils to international institutions.) How much room for manoeuvre does the government allow for social action by people in poverty and by particular interest groups? How can women or men from specific social groups shape the agenda and the decisions? If they can do so at community level, what happens to this participation at national and international levels? Finally, how would more and better participation improve outcomes for people in poverty? Researching these and other related questions has the potential to lead to action which improves the quality of human lives, by strengthening the accountability of public institutions to the individuals, families, and communities whom they serve.

Articles here consider the denial of citizenship rights from a gender perspective, and examine the relationship between gender inequality and political participation (not only in formal politics, but via activism in non-government organisations and community groups). Writers come from a range of backgrounds, including development funding organisations and community-based organisations in the global South, such as women's organisations, and teaching and training institutions. All are committed to the idea of active citizenship, in which individuals are at liberty to contribute their skills and knowledge to society through participating in public decision making which is relevant to their lives.

This short introduction looks at three key ways in which citizenship has been understood, before considering how citizenship fits into development. The introduction then highlights some ways in which citizenship fails women and men from minority or migrant groups. Finally, some strategies for securing full citizenship rights are considered.

Understandings of citizenship

Both rights and obligations are implicit in the concept of citizenship. The emphasis on citizens having obligations to their state can be traced back to ancient Greece, the birthplace of democracy. The cities of Greece were governed by participatory democracies. Men were citizens, and were required to participate directly in governance. However, women were not citizens; they were excluded from the system, together with children and slaves.

A different view of citizenship came from Europe and the USA in the seventeenth and eighteenth centuries. This emphasised citizens' right to make a range of claims on the state in which they lived. All citizens were guaranteed equal rights to make such claims, and impartial treatment before the law. Rights included civil rights, which were concerned with the freedom to speak, think, and worship as one wished, to be in control of one's own body, and to own property. Civil rights were also concerned with the right to enforce and defend all these principles through the legal system. Political rights were concerned with the right to participate in politics. There was no acknowledgement of the possibility that social inequalities between particular groups of people – for example, between women and men – might compromise or contradict the ideal of equal rights before the law.

A third view of citizenship, which is particularly relevant to our concerns in this collection of articles, comes from an influential twentieth-century theorist, T.H. Marshall. Marshall considered that equal rights and duties as citizens are what make people 'full members of a community' (Marshall 1950, 14, quoted in Yuval-Davis 1997, 69). Marshall also stressed the importance of social rights, as well as civil and political rights. He defined social rights as: 'the whole range from the right to a modicum of economic welfare and security to the right to share… in … social heritage and to live the life of a civilised being according to the standards [of] society' (Marshall 1950, 10). This view of citizenship takes our focus beyond the concerns of politics, national government, and legal systems, to consider individual people's interactions with collective groupings at all levels of society. These range from village councils allocating land and resolving marital disputes, to the international bodies which shape macro-economic policy and prosecute war crimes.

Where does citizenship fit into development?

Why is citizenship currently attracting so much attention from development policy makers and planners? For many, citizenship is a new 'lens' through which to see a very familiar set of concerns. Marshall's vision of citizenship is strikingly similar to the vision of empowerment through awareness raising and popular participation that has been promoted since the 1970s by development organisations. A focus on citizenship from the point of view of people in poverty invites us to consider the extent to which poor people are able to participate in the decision-making structures which shape events and outcomes in their own lives.

While this development model used to be seen as an alternative to dominant models of economic development, elements of it appear now to have been absorbed into the mainstream. Since the start of the new century, the atmosphere in international financial institutions and international development agencies seems to have changed. The international development establishment is pinning its faith on the power of elected governments, and the committed citizens whom they serve, to deliver development. The emphasis is no longer on the technical economic 'fixes' of the past 20 years. Structural adjustment programmes demanded that countries deregulated their markets and 'rolled back' state services. In contrast, lenders and development donors are now stressing the role of good governance in economic growth with poverty alleviation. Development programmes focusing on good governance include various measures to reform government structures to make them more efficient and more accountable, and consulting elements of civil society as part of national-level planning procedures. How genuine is this new commitment to accountability and participation? And what difference will it actually make in the lives of women and men in poverty? There is as yet no clear consensus on these questions.

The limits of citizenship

If governance is to be genuinely 'good', its institutions need to serve, and be accountable to, everyone who lives within a particular state. The idea of citizenship is that it is universal, encompassing everyone, regardless of sex, race, class, age, or creed (Lister 1997). In reality, however, citizenship fails to live up to the ideal. Researchers are currently engaged in charting the impact of this failure on the rights of women and minority groups, and policy makers and planners are developing programmes to bring about positive change.

Citizenship rights are not universal

Obviously, people living in countries with non-democratic systems of government do not have full citizenship rights. But even countries whose systems of government are democratic face serious challenges in putting the vision of universal citizenship rights into practice. If everyone is to be able to claim his or her rights, laws and administrative institutions need to aim for equality of outcome, rather than assuming – wrongly – that everyone is starting from a position of equality. This means reforming the law, and the systems of governance.

In global terms, women are the biggest group of people who are denied full citizenship rights. In some countries, women are denied citizenship outright. In others, women are declared in the constitution to be full and equal citizens, but the laws – in particular those dealing with issues of family and inheritance – often contradict and undermine national and international commitments to equality. Feminist studies of human rights, the law, and institutions have shown us that these are the products of decades or centuries of debate and decision making. They are founded on the age-old stereotype of men as actors in public life and governance, representing the interests of all family members. The corresponding stereotype of women is that they are dependent on a (benevolent) male household head. This means that women have no independent status enabling them to make claims on resources, or to appeal to the state for protection or support. Such laws, and the governance systems which enact them, reflect the world visions of the elite groups of men in middle life who first brought them into being.

Modernising these laws and systems is an enormous challenge – in particular, because women are still marginalised from participation in politics and governance. Many countries (both developing and post-industrialised) have now succeeded in passing progressive constitutions which honour women as full citizens, yet laws remain on the statute books which prevent women from exercising this equal status.

In her article, Lina Abou-Habib shows how the assumption that the man represents the entire family, and passes citizenship on to his children, has resulted in citizenship (and its associated rights) being denied to children born to national mothers and foreign fathers, in seven Arab countries. In turn, Mona Laczo discusses the experience of women in Nepal, including refugees and trafficked women. In her article, Kanchan Sinha discusses instances in which women from particular groups in India cannot use national laws to uphold the equal citizenship that they enjoy according to the Constitution. Women from marginalised groups with distinct cultural identities may be prevented from using the law by arguments that the state is wrong to impose universal notions of justice and legal rights, but should instead respect the rights of minority groups to dispense justice as they see fit.

Some groups of men, too, lack citizenship rights. One such group is migrants, who may be explicitly denied citizenship, or have only a diminished set of citizenship rights. Throughout history, millions of migrants have left their countries of origin in search of temporary or permanent work, or as a result of war and persecution. Now, however, rich countries are tightening their controls on migration across their borders, by preventing the citizens of poor countries from travelling there to visit family or seek employment in today's globalised economy. Illegal immigrants live in constant insecurity in many countries, unable to make basic claims for food, shelter, or health care from the state. Legal immigrants must usually wait for years to earn the right to apply for naturalisation as a citizen. In the meantime, as Lina Abou-Habib illustrates in her article, they contribute to the surrounding society but do not have the right to claim essential support and services from the state.

Barriers prevent some from 'active citizenship'

In theory, every citizen has an equal right to participate in decision making. For example, in a representative democracy, all citizens have the right to vote. However, if this right to participate is to be realised for all – women as well as men, people from minority groups as well as those from the dominant one – formal and informal measures are needed to cut through a complex mesh of economic, social, and cultural factors which entangle women, and people from marginalised groups, preventing them from entering public office.

For women, this means recognising that everyday life already presents women – and particularly women in poverty – with a heavy (and usually unequal) workload of income generation, food provision, child care, and household work. This in itself prevents many women from adopting a public role. In addition, it means challenging the spoken and unspoken prejudices that keep women out of public life. Many men, and some women, believe that women are unsuited for leadership and political participation. Deb Johnson, Hope Kabuchu, and Santa Vusiya Kayonga assessed the use of affirmative action in Uganda's Local Councils. They found that after women reached office, action was needed to equip them for the new roles, and to begin to break down the prejudices against them that were prevalent among their fellow councillors and the wider community.

The fact that formal political participation carries a heavy price for women means that they may choose a different form of active citizenship, outside formal politics. As Ruth Lister notes, 'for many women, involvement in community organisations or social movements can be more potentially fruitful than engagement in formal politics, which is often more alienating than empowering' (Lister 1997, 31). In any case, the line between politics and community involvement may well be blurred. In her article, Angela Coyle points out that both governments and international donors now increasingly recognise women's organisations as key actors in the promotion of women's rights, democracy, and citizenship. This is in line with the vision (outlined earlier) of good governance and a strong civil society as key elements in successful national development. However, Coyle argues that the experience of women's organisations in many different contexts belies donor commitment to civil society: sustained financial support and capacity building is needed. She describes a capacity-building project with four Polish women's organisations working to advance the interests of women in this former communist state.

Citizenship cannot alleviate poverty or inequality

A final criticism of the concept of citizenship is that it cannot guarantee a life of dignity, because dignity depends on freedom from economic want. Citizenship is of limited use in the fight against poverty caused by current national and international economic policies.

First, this is because citizenship focuses on civil and political rights, at the expense of economic rights. Over the past 20 years, women – and in particular women from developing countries – have pointed out that the range of rights recognised as legitimate by governments and international decision-making bodies needs to be joined by economic rights, if inequality, poverty, and suffering are to be addressed and eradicated (Sen and Grown 1987). Yet the issue of economic rights remains off the agenda; the maximum that seems to be envisaged is that civil society is involved in consultation exercises on poverty, as in the PRSP (Poverty Reduction Strategy Paper) process, led by the World Bank (Zuckerman 2002).

Second, citizenship focuses on the state. Historically, states in developing countries have not been able to respond to people's need for stable and sustainable livelihoods, because of the unfair terms on which their economies are incorporated into the global system. Currently, economic globalisation is further limiting the power of individual states to protect the livelihoods and human rights of their inhabitants. Many states are

'caught in a pincer movement between the forces of "globalisation" and localism/regionalism' (Lister 1997, 42). In her article on citizenship in Rio de Janeiro, Joanna Wheeler argues that people have developed a 'privatised citizenship' in response to economic crisis and neo-liberal policies which have no popular support. Growing poverty has led to an 'accompanying informalisation of political activity, as drug-related violence has further eroded the link between poor communities and formal democratic mechanisms' (Wheeler, this issue). Wheeler found that ideas of citizenship have shifted from a focus on formal political participation to an emphasis on family and community survival through self-help initiatives.

The idea of global citizenship leads us to focus on the responsibilities of rich countries towards countries which are impoverished enough not to be able to translate international principles of human rights into citizenship rights (Lister 1997). It also leads to a focus on the action of global civil society to ensure equal rights for citizens worldwide. Social movements, including the women's movement, and non-government organisations, are instrumental in this.

In their article, Jayashree Inbaraj, Subbalakshmi Kumar, Hellen Sambili, and Alison Scott-Baumann discuss the idea of global citizenship, from their perspectives as educationalists on three continents. Education for global citizenship is a radical approach to education which will potentially create widespread demand for international democratic decision making. It aims to develop moral sensibility in children through educating them about the wider world, and their own roles as world citizens (Oxfam GB 2003). The idea is to encourage the next generation to behave with a sense of responsibility, not only to themselves and their nation, but to the wider global community, and render children aware of their ability to challenge social, economic, and political injustice.

Conclusion

Citizenship is a contract between an individual and the society in which he or she lives. But in order to make use of that contract, individuals must be able to take part in shaping the society in which they live. This means that they need awareness of their political, economic, and social rights, and the rights of others. Further, they need to be confident that there are efficient ways of securing their rights, and that they can hold institutions and organisations accountable.

Throughout the world, until very recently, the sense of entitlement that is a key element of citizenship has tended to be restricted to men and dominant social groups. The impact of this fact on women and marginalised categories of people has been enormous. Deprived of a direct claim on the governments of the states in which they live, they have been unable to assert their right to equal treatment, and the state has been able to ignore its obligations to them.

Citizenship potentially provides a framework which enables all people to participate in political life at all levels: from the village to the state parliament, and beyond that to the global community. Its potential for liberation is enormous. Citizenship is about the relationship of an individual to the state in which he or she lives, and to wider society. Possessing rights as a citizen, and being aware of this, is an essential prerequisite to mounting a challenge to community, national, and international institutions which determine access to resources.

References

Lister, R. (1997) *Citizenship: Feminist Perspectives*, Basingstoke: Palgrave Macmillan

Marshall, T.H. (1950) *Citizenship and Social Class*, Cambridge: Cambridge University Press

Oxfam GB (2003) 'Global Citizenship', www.oxfam.org.uk/coolplanet/teachers/globciti/whatis.htm (last checked by the author 17 November 2003)

Sen, G. and C. Grown (1987) *Development, Crises and Alternative Visions: Third World Women's Perspectives*, New York: Monthly Review Press

Yuval-Davis, N. (1997) *Gender and Nation*, London: Sage Publications

Zuckerman, E. (2002) '"Engendering" Poverty Reduction Strategy Papers (PRSPs): the issues and the challenges', *Gender and Development* 10(3): 88-94

Women in Ugandan local government:
the impact of affirmative action

Deb Johnson with Hope Kabuchu and Santa Vusiya Kayonga

Uganda has introduced affirmative action to ensure that women are represented on the various Councils which govern village affairs. This article asks what has changed as a result of women's presence on the Councils. Both women and men felt that women had not significantly influenced Local Council planning and budget decisions. They felt this was due to lack of exposure to, and understanding of, council procedures and subjects (such as planning, budgeting, and accounting). However, women's presence in local government is leading to a positive change in men's and women's attitudes to women leaders in the community. These attitudes have previously prevented women's involvement in community activities. While this is positive in itself, the ability of women to participate actively in decisions about resource allocation needs to be monitored and supported – at both local and national government levels.

'Men will no longer be talking in 20 years. Museveni has given too much power to women.'
(Male sub-county Executive Committee member, Uganda)

In 1995, Uganda took a bold step to protect and enforce the rights of groups of people who had been marginalised in previous government systems. It included an affirmative-action clause within its new Constitution, which ran as follows: 'Notwithstanding anything in this Constitution, the State shall take affirmative action in favour of groups marginalised on the basis of gender, age, disability or any other reasons created by history, tradition or custom, for the purpose of redressing imbalances which exist against them' (Article 32.1).

The Constitution outlines the specific rights of women, as one of the marginalised groups noted above. This commitment to affirmative action and redressing past imbalances has offered an opportunity for Ugandan women that does not exist in many countries – developed and underdeveloped alike.

Although the Constitution provided an opening for women in the national policy environment, it did not provide guidance on how to put this commitment to affirmative action into practice in government institutions. The passing of the Local Government Act in 1997 laid the foundation for women's inclusion in the government's decision-making structures, by specifying that women councillors must form one-third of the membership of local government councils, and stipulating a minimum number of women appointees on many of the local government statutory commissions and committees. The implementation of these clauses was quickly put into effect at the local government elections in 1998.

Closely complementing the affirmative-action clause is the central government's commitment to decentralisation of administrative, political, and financial responsibility and authority to lower levels of government. Decentralisation has brought some of the decision making about government services closer to the people who use them. The local government system is now based on a five-tiered Local Council structure. Local Council 1 (LC1) refers to the village administrative structure. (The urban structure is similar, but we do not specifically examine it in this article.) This is the basic rural administrative and political unit in Uganda. The LC1 Executive Committee is a village governance committee elected by the village council, which consists of all residents of the village aged over 18. The next tiers of Local Council are LC2 (parish level, covering several villages); LC3 (sub-county); LC4 (county); and finally LC5 (district).

Since women are generally more comfortable in, and less constrained from, getting involved in community affairs which are very close to home, moving decision making closer to the village level should offer them a better opportunity to influence local development, and give them a platform from which to move into higher positions with more responsibilities. Like men, women can run for public office of a mixed constituency, with the chance thereby of being elected to represent everyone, not just women. In addition, there are seats set aside specifically for women, in order to assure at least one-third representation of women on the Councils. These women are now elected by universal adult suffrage, even though they are elected to represent women specifically.

This article examines the impact of the measures outlined above on the work of the Local Councils, and on attitudes to women's role in governance. It is derived from work done for a five-country study commissioned by the Belgian government[1] and organised by the Special Evaluator for International Co-operation (working directly under the Belgian parliament), in the context of an overall thematic evaluation on poverty reduction. The study relied largely on qualitative, rather than quantitative, methods of analysis. Semi-structured interviews were carried out with 23 district politicians and staff from the two districts

involved in the project. Two sub-counties in each district were selected for their different characteristics. At this level, focus-group discussion and analysis approaches were used with 16 lower-level Local Councils (LC1 and LC2), and approximately 18 different community groups (such as credit, farmers, women, youth, and functional adult literacy groups). Sixteen women councillors at different levels were interviewed about their personal and professional histories.

Factors affecting women in political leadership

Legal and policy environment

In Uganda, affirmative action for women, youth, and people with disabilities, within the Local Government Act of 1997, and subsequent bills and laws,[2] has rapidly changed the decision-making environment, opening up opportunities for women in particular. In our research, we asked about legislation that has supported women to go into politics. The most commonly cited pieces of legislation were the Constitution and the Local Government Act. In discussions specifically about women's rights, the Land Act is noted, since it has a particular provision concerning the right of women and dependent children to land.

Affirmative action has been further strengthened by the appointment of a woman as national Vice-President, and the vocal and visible actions of several women members of parliament.

Institutional structure

Legislation and written policies supporting women's involvement in the political decision-making sphere are undermined somewhat by the lack of support for the relevant ministry and district departments tasked with creating an environment which encourages women's political participation. Bearing in mind the strong legal and policy commitment to women's empowerment in Uganda, the limited commitment of resources to the institutions that are responsible for ensuring the inclusion of women in decision making is confusing, and seemingly contradictory.

A central ministry responsible for women's issues was established in 1988. Since then the ministry has undergone several changes of name and strategy, including a shift from a Women in Development (WID) focus towards a Gender and Development (GAD) focus. Currently, the national-level institution for policy development on gender is the Ministry of Gender, Labour, and Social Development (MGLSD). The corresponding structure within the districts is the Community Development Department (CDD). The CDD is much more involved than the Ministry in the implementation of development initiatives in the districts, through its efforts to create awareness of development issues within communities, and to mobilise them to address blockages to development.

Both the Ministry and the Community Services Departments[3] at the district level are perpetually under-resourced in all aspects – human, financial, information, and material. There are competent people within the Ministry and the district departments, but they are hampered by this overall lack of resources, and by the lack of a clear mandate to make strategic decisions about the vast array of responsibilities expected of them. The lack of resources greatly hinders the Ministry and the Community Services Departments from implementing some key policies and strategies (for example, the National Gender Policy of 1997, and the National Action Plan on Women 1999/2000 to 2003/04).

Social and cultural context

The nomination of a woman Vice-President has set a precedent in the Local Councils, some of which have taken this to be a general rule. Several men in our research said that if a man is elected as the Chairperson, then the Vice-Chairperson of a Local Council must be a woman.

Some people noted that they heard of the need for gender balance and gender equality through the radio. Both men and women specifically mentioned radio presentations by the MGLSD, as well as specific news stories. Some had heard about affirmative action through the newspapers. Some noted that it is the women in parliament who raise difficult and contentious issues, and challenge the President and others, when they feel that things are not right.

Others said they had heard about the need for gender sensitivity and balance through materials and workshops organised for members of various committees, such as the Parish Land Committees. The Land Committees had received specific materials about women's and children's rights (from the MGLSD, non-government organisations, and other donors), which were intended to help them to understand the parts of Ugandan law that supersede traditional or customary rules.

Blockages to women entering political leadership

The people we spoke to in rural areas identified a number of factors which, in their view, blocked women from assuming leadership positions. These factors highlight the struggle that women face in maintaining 'traditional' roles (reproductive/domestic responsibilities) and creating new, community/political roles for themselves.

Women's lack of skills

We were told that women are afraid and shy to contribute to Local Council deliberations. This fear and shyness is rooted in three main influences: limited command of language; cultural factors which discourage women's participation; and inexperience, which causes lack of understanding of Councils and how they operate.

Limited command of language is a problem for many of the women elected to Local Councils. While they have some level of formal education, they are frequently not comfortable using technical or conceptual language. Many of the women interviewed from the lower Local Councils said that they were not comfortable with some of the concepts of local governance, and the technical language used within Council discussions. They attributed this discomfort to their relative lack of exposure to new ideas and procedures found outside the village, in comparison with the men elected to the Council. In some cases, the fact that Council meetings use English creates problems.

Cultural barriers prevent women speaking assertively in mixed company. We observed during our interviews that many times women were not able to make effective contributions in meetings – they hesitated slightly before making their point, or spoke quietly, which allowed a more vocal and aggressive participant to talk over them. This may be connected to cultural issues. Women in many parts of Uganda are not supposed to express their ideas openly in public. Women in the assessment reported that even in the home there is a limit to the amount of discussion or dialogue that a woman can have with her husband. This was expressed more commonly amongst the Banyoro, Baganda, Bagungu, and Bakiga people to whom we spoke.

Another factor creating shyness was a lack of understanding of Councils. With the passing of the Local Government Act of 1997, and then the implementation of the affirmative-action clauses in the local government elections in 1998, women were thrust into Local Council positions, with little or no preparation for their roles and responsibilities. In some cases, villagers had to cajole and plead with women to stand for office, just to fill some of the spaces created. The number of women who had been exposed to experiences which stood them in good stead for this was very small, compared with the number of experienced men. Often, women who had retired or been retrenched from the civil service, or who had retired from business, were asked by their communities to take Council positions.

The majority of the councillors interviewed (both men and women) said that they had not been trained in these new roles. They said they learned about their roles and responsibilities through radio programmes, and through news stories concerning the expectations of local governments. However, women's access (in terms of time and ownership of radios) to radio programmes and other forms of political sensitisation has been questioned (UWONET 1998). Queries have also been raised about mental barriers to listening to this kind of programme: women may simply lack interest, thinking that these issues are not relevant to them (ibid.).

Another skill lacked by many women was knowing how to ride a bicycle. Since some of the posts in the Local Councils require the candidate to travel distances to visit her constituency, she must use a bicycle, as other forms of transport are less common and more expensive. In districts such as Kibaale, many women do not know how to ride bicycles, or there are cultural beliefs that discourage them. One of the more interesting sayings we discovered was that if a woman rides a bicycle, then rats will eat the seat. In Hoima district, bicycle riding by women was more common and considered less of a barrier to women taking up posts.

Objections to travelling and working late at night

Women members of Councils must have the freedom to be away from the home for extended periods of time during the day, and sometimes well into the evening. We were told by sub-county councillors in Nkooko: 'Men do not want women travelling, especially if they were staying out late into the evening'. Even in discussions with councillors in Hoima, the issue of women travelling in the evenings was still difficult for their husbands to accept. This was cited in one village as a key reason why women were not being considered for the position of Chairperson. Villagers said that men refuse to let their wives go out of the house after dark. They did not state the reasons clearly; it was repeated frequently in group discussions and individual interviews that women councillors will 'misbehave'.

Statements about women 'misbehaving' were quickly followed by observations that the Museveni government has given too much freedom to women. Respondents reasoned that this excess freedom can be seen in the increasing number of women who 'misbehave' in public as well as in the home. Definitions of 'misbehaviour' came not only from men (young, old, married, and unmarried), but also from some older women. A woman who 'misbehaves' does not wash her husband's clothes, does not prepare meals for her husband, or does not follow the instructions of her husband as head of the family. One of the older women added that these women do not wear traditional clothing and hairstyles.

Objections to travelling and working late at night are usually mitigated when the woman is bringing earnings into the home. Men would acknowledge that experience has demonstrated that if a women is given a chance to earn an income then she will 'uplift the standards' of the family.

Women's domestic and reproductive responsibilities

These responsibilities were perceived by respondents as by far the most common factors limiting women's involvement in local government. The specific reasons given by respondents included: 'It is our culture for women to be at home', and 'Women must take care of the children'.

A female LC3 representative noted that women are torn between the opportunity to play a stronger role in community politics, and the social expectation that they will continue to play their traditional reproductive roles as wives and mothers. We found that being married seems to be seen as a prerequisite for a woman to be considered as a candidate for Local Councils at the lower levels (LC1 and LC2).

Nkooko sub-county councillors (both male and female) linked the idea of women needing to take care of the children to the prevailing lack of family planning, which results in larger families. The total fertility rate (the number of children that a woman will have in her reproductive lifetime) is high for women in Uganda, at 6.9 (UNDP 1999). This means a greater workload for women, resulting in less time for pursuing activities outside the family.

Men's fears over gender power relations

The quotation that heads this article typifies men's fears that women's power will surpass their own, and women will become richer or stronger. Men fear that new-found independence (derived from earning income or from political participation) will encourage women to leave their husbands. For many men, women's independence means that they will no longer *need* men, and hence will leave the marital home and return to their home village and their parents.

While this fear was, once again, associated with women 'misbehaving', it was also linked to a more basic concern that men are losing their own roles and identities, while women discover new roles and responsibilities. Closely related to this view was a concern about the power relations within the household. Men said that they would become the laughing-stock of their village if their wives were seen to be the heads of the households.

Age restrictions on older women's participation in politics

The common view is that women over the age of 60 should not become involved in politics. One older man from Kakindo village in Hoima district said that this was because they would neglect to take care of their husbands in their old age, but he would accept their involvement if the Council paid them a salary. (These are voluntary positions, but there are ways of getting some compensation through allowances.) In addition, older women are shouldering the responsibility of taking care of their AIDS-orphaned grandchildren. Men, on the other hand, can get involved in politics at any age without any age-related restrictions, since in general their responsibilities lessen as they get older. They are supported by a pension, by the investments they made earlier in life (for example, in agriculture or business), or by their children.

Qualities needed to become a woman councillor

Some qualities appear fairly consistently in the histories and backgrounds of a number of women currently holding elected posts in the Councils and holding positions of power within the Executive Committees of these Councils. Although local councillors frequently talked of the involvement of women in the Councils as an inevitable outcome of laws passed recently by the government, the standard and qualifications demanded of women are quite different from those demanded of men.

Generally, women have to satisfy higher standards than men if they are to be elected to office. This was summed up in the statement by a male district Executive Committee member, who said, 'Men are passed through [to office in Councils] by cultural standards, whereas women pass through on merit'.

Previous exposure
The women elected to the Local Councils and appointed to Executive Committees are, or have been, engaged in many visible activities outside their homes. In one LC2 Executive Committee, the Chairman said that he chose three women for his Executive Committee because they had been exposed to ideas and ways of life outside the parish.

The issue of previous exposure of this kind was not considered so important for men. Study participants from the Isongero Trading Centre, Imara village in Kibaale district, said that men have more opportunities and freedom to travel outside the village, or spend time listening to radio and talking to people within the markets and trading centres; therefore most people assume that they are sufficiently exposed to external issues and realities.

Formal education
The election of a woman to the position of the Vice-Chairperson in one village was attributed to the fact that she had been through seven years of schooling, could speak English, and was 'presentable' (that is, she gave a good impression of her village through her appearance and manner). This particular woman was said to be poor, and was not a member of a community group such as a women's group or a credit group. It seemed to respondents that it was the woman's educational background and English-language skills that had made her an attractive candidate for the Local Council.

In contrast, the Chairman of the same Council did not have any formal education, or English-language skills. However, he was a wealthy businessman in the village. One villager said that the woman had been elected 'to give the Chairperson ... someone who is educated'. There were other cases where business success was a more important factor than formal education when electing a local councillor, but nonetheless a lack of formal education is considered to be a stigma, especially higher up in the Local Council system.

Financial security
Much financial success in rural areas starts with the production and sale of agricultural goods. As women frequently lack access and control over the means and uses of agricultural production, this has generally limited their ability to become wealthy. However, there are three main reasons why political candidates require a constant and steady source of income. The first reason is

the cost of political campaigning. Men and women alike talked of what they perceived as the enormous financial costs involved in campaigning. For many, campaigning meant offering something tangible to people in their constituency. It could mean providing local beer or other alcohol to men, whereas women constituents might be given a bar of soap, a packet of salt, or some other household item. In addition to being able to afford to give these things to voters, candidates need to be able to travel widely and frequently throughout their constituency, to build their awareness of local concerns.

Three female district councillors from Kibaale said that women actively campaigning for positions at the district level generally require both a supportive husband (for financial support and to create a good image), and a good supplemental source of income. This is where women face a greater challenge than men, because women are expected to be supportive of their husbands' ambitions, whatever they may be. The reverse has not often been the case.

Councillors also need money to enable them to function on a daily basis. Most of the positions in the lower Councils are voluntary, their occupants only receiving some money for 'sitting' (meeting attendance) and/or 'night' allowances (money intended to cover lodging costs when travelling), and possibly some money for transport or other direct Council-related costs.

For some councillors, especially those at lower levels of government, the sitting allowance is seen as a source of income for the household, to offset the time contributed. In other positions with more responsibilities, which are more time-consuming, the sitting allowance is not enough to offset the lost income for the individual involved. If a councillor does not have sufficient income to enable him or her to weather this, problems will arise.

Since reproductive work is unpaid, and women's income-generating activities typically bring in low returns, the allowances may make Local Council work economically attractive. Men and women in the districts stated that if women are making some money from their involvement in lower-level Local Council work, men are more willing to ignore the cultural barriers to women's participation in politics, and allow female relatives to become active.

Although we did not specifically focus on this in our evaluation, there is evidence that many women could not contest Council seats because they could not raise the registration fee (UWONET 1998). UWONET (the Uganda Women's Network) further notes that women would rather spend their limited, hard-earned money on their children's school fees than on campaigning.

Specific skills appropriate to Council work

Women involved in civil-service positions are appointed to what seem to be positions requiring similar skills on Executive Committees. For example, a clerk/typist is appointed to the post of General Secretary, an agricultural extension worker is appointed to the post of Secretary for Production, or a woman involved in management of group funds is appointed to the post of Secretary of Finance.

Experiences and examples of women representatives

The mandatory requirement of ensuring that at least one-third of Council members are women had been translated slightly differently in each district. In Hoima district, four women's constituencies were established, to ensure the one-third minimum representation on the District Council. At the sub-county level, the district set up women's constituencies to ensure that approximately one man and one woman from each parish were elected to the LC3.

From our discussions in the two districts, we felt that the people to whom we talked are content to have women elected to the minimum number of mandatory seats in the Council, leaving men to compete for the regular constituency seats (based on electing leaders to represent a specific geographic and population size). In Hoima, there was only one woman who campaigned against men for a regular constituency post, and she campaigned for, but eventually lost, the position of Chairperson of LC5. In Kibaale district, however, three women were elected to regular constituency seats – two of whom competed against men and won. The reasons for the difference cannot be explained at this point, but the result is that women hold 47 per cent of the District Council seats in Kibaale, as opposed to the minimum level of 33 per cent found in Hoima.

Discussions with Executive Committee members of each District Council revealed that the women councillors in Kibaale's Executive Committee (where women make up 46 per cent of the posts, compared with only 14 per cent in Hoima) have made a significant and clearly visible impact in their constituencies, lobbying (successfully) for public funds to be invested in development activities in their constituencies.

Several times, men and women referred to what they said was a commonly held perception that women are more caring – a characteristic attributed to women's maternal nature – and that they are more transparent and honest in financial management. When asked where these perceptions of care, transparent dealing, and honesty come from, the majority of group members (non-politicians) who participated in the study talked of the positive experiences that they had had. For example, women were widely said to be more responsible than men in the management of household money. Participants pointed out the fact that there had not been many negative experiences with women in the parliament or other positions of power. This went beyond their direct experience at the community level: they indicated that there have been few scandals reported in the newspapers or on the radio that involved women in power. It was also pointed out that the more well-known women (at the national and district levels) have promoted specific causes that are good for the entire country, such as the exposure of corruption and the promotion of children's rights.

Outcomes from women's involvement in local government

There was a mix of opinions about the contributions and effectiveness of women on the Councils.

Women's influence over budget decisions

Some male councillors said that increasing the number of women on the Councils has improved the allocation of funds, because women lobby for facilities which benefit everyone (such as health facilities), and for money to support women to get involved in household and community development activities. Once they are elected to the Council, the objective of most women is first to increase the amount of money going to the women's vote. The women's vote at LC3 and LC5 levels is used to mobilise and sensitise women on a whole range of issues affecting them, such as maintenance of the home, health issues (for example, immunisation and nutrition of children), and establishing home gardens. This mobilisation and sensitisation can entail women councillors holding meetings with women in the village, or it can mean getting interested, engaged women to visit other areas of the district and beyond.

However, both women and men felt that the lack of exposure to, and understanding of, the Council procedures and subjects (such as planning, budgeting, and accounting) have, so far, prevented women from significantly influencing Local Council outputs and making a greater impact on budget decisions. The Kibaale district councillors interviewed felt that some of the quieter women councillors in Kibaale district were easily swayed in their decisions, depending on who was lobbying them at the time. They thought this was connected to their lack of confidence in Council matters, linked both to limited exposure and/or understanding, and to cultural influences.

Challenges to women's right to participate in budget decisions

Perceptions of women's right to participate in Council budget decisions were connected to their perceived contribution to graduated tax. In Uganda, graduated tax is levied on every man over the age of 18 years. The level is calculated on the basis of household assets. It is important to note that most men pay their graduated tax requirements through the sale of agricultural products.

Until recently, women's contributions to household income, or their central role in agricultural production, were not often considered to be significant contributions to the upkeep of the household. The results of women's agricultural efforts are generally not quantified, since women grow subsistence crops and provide family labour for cash crops. A woman's contribution to the household is, therefore, not considered as important as a man's contribution, because he is generating cash (through the sale of cash crops) for household requirements that need money, such as school fees and graduated tax. By disregarding women's contribution to cultivating and harvesting, one can more easily disregard a woman's contribution to household income, and hence to payment of graduated tax.

The fact that women's contribution to the household is not often understood to be an indirect contribution to the payment of graduated tax leads men to justify the exclusion of women from local government planning. Men in our research used statements such as: 'They don't pay for g-tax

[graduated tax], so they don't really have a right to make decisions about the 25 per cent [the village's percentage of local government revenue]'. It is also possible that women may dismiss their own right to participate in discussions about local revenue, which is primarily graduated tax revenue.

Men are not openly and actively using the payment of graduated tax to prevent women's access to the local government planning and allocation process. However, if a non-taxpayer advocates action which is unpopular to a taxpayer, she or he can be dismissed as having no entitlement to make such decisions. A male villager noted an example where an old man who had been exempted from paying graduated tax was ridiculed by the councillors during a lower-level Council meeting, when he tried to disagree with how funds were being spent.

The impact of women's presence on Local Council Courts

One of the more positive impacts coming from the mandatory reservation, for women, of at least one-third of the seats on the local government councils in Uganda was their presence on the Local Council Courts, specifically the LC1 Courts. The local court is formed from the Local Council Executive Committee. It is the first forum for conflict mediation within the Local Council system, and should be the most accessible. Accessibility depends largely on the people on the LC1 Executive Committee. If they are approachable (both in terms of availability and personality), and if they seem to be fair and honest in their decision-making capacity, then people say that the Court works well. If they are not seen as fair, honest, or approachable, then there are few avenues for recourse, as few villagers have the financial capacity and confidence to bypass the LC1 Courts to seek redress in higher courts.

The research revealed an interesting contrast between opinions on women's involvement in the Local Council meetings and on their involvement in the Local Courts. Both men and women agreed that women were more comfortable and better acquainted with the Local Courts than with the Local Councils. One woman councillor summarised the reasons: 'We [women] are used to village issues. We know what is happening in the village. The Council is the introduction of new ideas. When people are mistreated [and come to the Courts], we naturally come to the rescue.'

Women and men, including local police officials, confirmed that there are more 'women's issues' being brought to the Courts. These issues were specifically stated as: lack of support by the husband for the children; domestic abuse; defilement (sexual abuse); and protection of widows' inheritance rights. Generally, domestic abuse cases involve the husband physically abusing his wife. Even though there are said to be cases of women verbally and physically abusing their husbands, especially when drunk, very few men would risk the humiliation of taking their wives to court over the abuse.

Conclusion

After local government elections in Uganda in 1998, many women were swept into politics without adequate preparation, in order to fill the one-third quota set out in the Local Government Act 1997. Given the short period of time since the local government elections, and the number of obstacles to effective local governance, the long-term impact of this increase in women's political involvement on the way in which Councils work and how they allocate funds is not yet clear. Despite the lack of conclusive evidence on women's impact on local government, some positive and negative changes are beginning to emerge.

There has been an expansion in the number of women on the Local Councils,

and this has increased women's confidence in, and use of, the Local Council Courts for 'women's issues' such as child and domestic abuse cases, and cases in which child support is sought.

It seems that women's involvement in national and local government Councils has increased the number of positive role models for women. This has encouraged other women to become more engaged in a variety of community activities, such as joining groups, campaigning for public office, and starting businesses. Positive female role models seem also to have had a significant impact on the attitudes of men.

However, having confident role models is only one side of the story. As discussed above, some women councillors are reluctant to express their thoughts or opinions during Council meetings. Their lack of confidence (or in some cases lack of interest) in speaking out, results in men (and some women) dismissing women's potential contribution. They are seen as easily swayed by other, more vocal, councillors. In many cases, women councillors are considered to be ineffective. While there are male councillors who are not active, there is a greater expectation that women should be more active, perhaps as a justification for affirmative action. When a woman is not playing an active role, some people are quick to conclude that women do not make good councillors, thereby making it more difficult for other women to follow.

There are also some changes due to women's participation in Local Councils which some believe to be negative. There is a lingering impression that women's increasing involvement in community activities will result in long-lasting changes in cultural norms and traditions. At the beginning of many of the discussions, the increased freedom of women (as evidenced through their participation in public life) was seen by both men and women as positive. Men talked of 'being relieved' of the burden of supporting the entire family alone. They would further note that, with the easing of this burden, they felt happier. However, soon after these initial thoughts, men turned to their perceptions of the negative impacts of women's freedom. Frequently these grew out of fears that their wives would become financially independent and leave them, or that they would become uncontrollable.

Men's self-image depends to a great extent on their having a productive role in society. Their ability to earn money and make decisions about its use sets them apart as the heads of households. As women start to move more strongly into productive *and* community roles, they threaten this male self-image. Men are unsure and worried about their place in the household and community, since women seem to have the capacity to pursue their own goals. Men expressed fears of high divorce rates; of women taking them to court to claim half of the household assets; and a dramatic increase in women 'misbehaving' (translated into women leaving them, especially women finding other men).

Not everyone perceived all changes to cultural norms and traditions as negative. One Local Council councillor said that changing negative cultural practices is actually good. He noted that, according to tradition, women were not supposed to eat chicken, but now everyone eats it, and this is a good and positive change. Yet he ended by saying that he was afraid that women's freedom would change even the good traditions: 'The food of a house girl does not taste as good as your own wife's food'.

Deb Johnson lived and worked in Uganda from 1997 until 2003 as a co-director of Sikiliza International, Ltd. She is currently working as a Local Government Advisor with SNV (a Dutch non-government organisation) in Honduras. djohn_98@yahoo.com

Hope Kabuchu lives and works in Uganda, based in Kampala. She has significant experience in gender mainstreaming and analysis, as well as skills in management and organisational issues of development project implementation, monitoring, and evaluation.

Santa Vusiya Kayonga lives and works in Uganda, based in Kampala. She has had extensive experience in mainstreaming gender issues into planning and evaluation of development projects. In addition, she has been involved in literacy and adult education through her work within the Ministry of Gender. nordic@africaonline.co.ug

Notes

1 However, the conclusions presented here do not represent the ideas and/or perceptions of the Government of Belgium. Any errors or false conclusions are the sole responsibility of the authors.
2 These include the Land Act of 1998; Local Government Finance and Accounting Regulations 1998; the Poverty Eradication Action Plan 2000; and the Domestic Relations Bill 1999.
3 The Community Services Departments are linked to the MGLSD and are given a large range of social-service responsibilities, such as promoting and organising functional adult literacy courses, enforcing labour regulations, gender sensitisation work, and other community mobilisation work.

References

UNDP (1998) *Uganda Human Development Report*, Kampala: UNDP

UWONET (1998) 'Women Emerging in Uganda's Democracy: A Documentation of Women's Experiences in Uganda's Local Council and Local Government Elections', Kampala: Ugandan Women's Network

Citizenship degraded:
Indian women in a modern state and a pre-modern society

Kanchan Sinha

Proverbial statements about women being second-class citizens are familiar in many societies. It is vitally important to challenge the many barriers to full citizenship that confront women, and barriers to women's human rights in general. Development interventions must help to do this. The denial of equal citizenship to women is a phenomenon familiar in many parts of the world, but it assumes alarming proportions in societies that are still largely 'pre-modern'. Development workers should not be deflected from addressing these issues because of sensitivities about not becoming involved in 'other' cultures and traditions. While these sensitivities are a welcome development in many ways, a blind eye should not be turned to the injustices and oppressions to which women are subjected. The development sector must devise effective strategies to deal with culturally sensitive issues, such as forging partnerships with indigenous social movements. This article draws on experience from India, illustrating its argument with three cases of violations of women's rights.

Citizenship is often seen exclusively as a political issue, but many of its facets go beyond the political domain. Citizens live in social relationships which are shaped by economic and social forces, as well as by politics. Gender, race, class, and religion are among the principal aspects of social relations that influence people's experience of citizenship. A current challenge to development workers is to decide whether and how their interventions should address cultural beliefs and practices which challenge the idea of women as equal to men, and hence undermine the idea that women are full citizens of the states in which they live.

Cultural beliefs and practices are sensitive matters, and more so in societies that are still largely 'pre-modern'. The reasons for this sensitivity go way back in history. In the case of India in the colonial era, the 'West' came to colonise the 'East', with pretensions of 'civilising' it. The colonials invented the suspect image of the 'Orient', to further their economic and political interests and designs. Nationalists challenged the colonial powers on two bases. First, strategies of mass mobilisation against the foreign rulers often relied on ideas of cultural identity, which were supported by cultural practices that were rooted in age-old traditions. Second, they claimed the right of the nation-state to sovereignty. This was inspired largely by exposure to Western ideals. Thus, there was an internal tension at the core of the nationalist movement: it deployed pre-modern culture in its struggle to attain the modern goal of a sovereign nation-state.

In India in the 1950s and 1960s, the emphasis shifted to modernising society, and building a modern nation-state, in the immediate aftermath of independence from British rule. This required challenging many of the cultural practices that had gone into forging a national identity during the anti-colonial struggle. Lawmakers who wrote the Constitution for a newly independent India had to tread cautiously, especially in the domain of the so-called personal laws. These laws about marriage, inheritance, and many other cultural-traditional practices had to accommodate the sensitivities of religious communities.

Today, the pendulum has swung away from the modernising ethos of half a century ago. These are times of heightened sensitivities about cultural identities and practices. Post-modern scholars from the West adopt an anthropologist's attitude towards cultural practices of a tradition-bound community. This attitude is reverential towards all existing cultures and traditions, and, at the same time, seeks to uncover deeply structured meanings and 'cultural reason' in the age-old practices. Post-colonial scholars from the East do not necessarily glorify everything in the 'native cultures'. However, they place the blame for disturbing aspects of these societies, such as communalism, caste-based hierarchy and discrimination, and even certain forms of gender-based oppression, at the doorstep of colonialism. For them, modernity is suspect, because of its association with colonialism.

It is interesting to note that these new perspectives have emerged in the era of globalisation. National barriers are being dismantled in the realms of finance, production, and trade, but in the realm of culture and social practice care is being taken (despite a certain degree of Americanisation) to preserve and attach value to all that has existed for centuries and millennia. It is hard to decide whether this originates in a genuine concern for cultural diversity and pluralism, or whether it is part of a strategy to facilitate the smooth globalisation of capital.

Culture, development, and globalisation of human rights

A certain kind of globalisation – of basic human rights, and of norms of equal citizenship for all – would be immensely desirable for women and for other oppressed communities, groups, and social classes. Because of this, the issue of 'cultural relativism'[1] is critically important for the development sector. As Radhika Coomaraswamy points out in her Report of the Special Rapporteur on Violence against Women to the Commission on Human Rights, United Nations: 'Cultural relativism is often used as an excuse to permit inhuman and discriminatory practices against women in the community, despite clear provisions in many human rights instruments, including the Convention on the Elimination of All Forms of Discrimination against Women…' (Coomaraswamy, 2002).

Not only the world economy, but also the development sector, is currently experiencing 'selective globalisation'. The development sector has a global institutional framework. The organisations and the functionaries who formulate development goals and strategies, and who command resources, are mostly from the developed countries of the North. However, the societies where these strategies and resources are deployed are mostly in the developing countries in the South. Under this arrangement there does not exist, at least so far, a mechanism of local democratic control from the South over the interventions that aim to 'develop' it. This obstructs the global development organisations from acquiring popular legitimacy in the societies where they make their development interventions. They remain aliens, always wary of the danger that their interventions in local culture will be seen as the return of the colonialists. This puts pressure on them to adopt pragmatic versions of cultural relativism.

In the remainder of this article, I will argue that cultural barriers to empowerment and emancipation are the most formidable obstacles to Indian women realising equal citizenship, and that development organisations need to respond by avoiding the trap of cultural relativism and by advocating women's human rights.

State, power, and culture

The formal legal structure of the Indian Constitution grants equal citizenship rights to women. Yet any statement about the Indian Constitution being largely gender-egalitarian in bestowing on men and women equal rights of citizenship would raise many eyebrows, if not unleash outright condemnation, in the Indian feminist movement. There are numerous reasons for objecting to any such statement.

Patriarchal character of personal laws

First, the Constitution has serious limitations, especially in the realm of personal laws. The patriarchal character of the Indian state has been, and continues to be, a live issue in the women's movement. As Nivedita Menon puts it: 'In the laws on rape and marriage, women's right to property, custody and guardianship of children, the Indian state shows itself to be the protector of patriarchal values. Marital rape is not recognised, and only penetration by the penis is considered to be rape, any other form of sexual assault however grievous, being considered a lesser crime. Feminists argue that this kind of under-standing of rape is clearly based on the value of women's chastity for patriarchal systems of property and descent, and has nothing to do with the notion of women as individuals with the right to bodily integrity. As for laws governing marriage and inheritance, religious communities have their own personal laws, and all of these discriminate against women. The Directive Principles of state policy call for the state to enact a uniform civil code, but successive govern-ments have not so far done so, because the personal laws are protected by the Fund-amental Right to freedom of religion. Some feminists see this as a prominent example of the way in which the state protects patriarchal interests' (Menon 1999, 16).

Sameness and difference

Another critique of the Indian Constitution sees the source of the problem in the reliance of the Constitution on formal, rather than substantive, ideas of equality.[2] The High Court and the Supreme Court interpret the principle of equality to be operative under the condition of *sameness*. Women, being *different*, do not necessarily have claims to equality. Furthermore, the difference is posited in the notion that women are weaker than men and, hence, in need of protection. Such an interpretation is deployed in selected areas of personal and social life, so that some laws are affected by it, while others are not – but the damage is done. This idea easily gets harnessed in the service of patriarchy. The substantive model of equality, on the other hand, would have taken into account the actual conditions of women's subordination, and would have used both the factors of *sameness* and *difference* in such a way that would work against the conditions of subordination.

The mismatch between justice and law

There are yet other critiques. Some people question the ability of the law to deliver universal justice.[3] They argue that ideas of justice depend on specific and particular moral visions that differ from community to community. Justice must, therefore, be culture-specific, singular, and unique. Law, on the other hand, must take a general form, uniformly applicable to all those who come under its purview. Within its domain of application, it must be universal. The problem is obvious, especially in the cases where many communities and cultures exist under one state. There is a mismatch between justice and law, which arises from the mismatch between the particular and the universal.

I do not necessarily disagree with most of these critiques, but I have a different approach to the issue. My focus is on the question: what prevents the formal rights enshrined in the Constitution from becoming real and substantive?

Culture as a barrier to realisation of formal rights

The Indian Constitution is not perfect: it does have patriarchal elements, and it is based on a formalist interpretation of equality which takes *sameness* as the deciding criterion. It cannot be denied, however, that it also contains the notion of equal citizenship. To take an obvious example, it gives every citizen the right to vote and elect a government on the basis of universal suffrage. While democracy is not enough, if conditions of social and economic inequality remain, democracy is a burning issue of rights and justice. An occurrence all too common in India, especially in the case of *Dalits* ('Untouchables'), is that members of an oppressed community are prevented by the local powers-that-be from casting their votes.

There are many layers of institutions and practices which prevent formal rights from becoming real. These layers must be analysed, and weakened or removed. The first layer consists of the parts of the Constitution itself that prevent the realisation of equal citizenship for women. We have seen the example of personal laws. The second layer consists of the interests and the entrenched power structure in the economy and in society. These present formidable barriers to the operation of the Constitution. The third layer consists of cultural practices within the community and the family. Nothing is immune from the influence of cultural beliefs and practices, and for this reason the other layers are not fully separable from the cultural one. Yet it needs to be examined in its own right. Cultural beliefs and practices cast a big shadow over the possibility of turning many of women's formal rights into real ones.

Power and culture are the two large-scale barriers to realisation of women's human rights. By power I mean the macro-level and institutional structures of power, whereas culture permeates the beliefs and practices of an entire society. My assertion is that culture is the more formidable obstacle to the realisation of Indian women's formal rights to equality, including the right to equal citizenship. Some unequal power relationships can be addressed relatively easily, by reforming the institutions in which they are played out. Cultural ideas of women as inferior to men, however, do not only play out in particular institutions, such as the family: they prevail throughout every aspect of life, in a fluid, uncontrollable form.

A number of feminist investigations of the Constitution and of the legal framework have come to similar conclusions. Vasudha Dhagamwar, for example, makes the following observation in her study of the Indian Penal Code: 'Criminal law also illustrates most vividly the problems that arise when social norms differ or contradict the provisions of the law. It has been found, almost universally, that in such cases social norms prevail… Not only the people, but the civil servants, police and judiciary are influenced by the social norms' (Dhagamwar 1992, 10).

Indian society is well known for cultural practices such as dowry, arranged marriages, and *sati* (the custom of self-immolation by widows on their husbands' funeral pyres). These have been the focus of heated debate among colonial, post-modern, and post-colonial scholars, and also among activists. Each one of these practices violates the basic human rights of women. Yet despite this, some argue that these practices were benign and even useful, in the organic culture that prevailed before the arrival of 'modernity' in India. I do not have space to examine arguments that romanticise the pre-British or the pre-Islamic India. Instead I will summarise three selected cases from more modern times which, in my opinion, shed clear light on the role of culture in degrading women's citizenship and in sanctifying the violation of their basic human rights.

How culture violates citizenship rights

The Shah Bano case[4]

In April 1985, the Supreme Court of India delivered a judgment granting a small maintenance allowance to a 73-year-old divorcée, Shah Bano, and ordering her ex-husband, Mohammed Ahmed Khan, to pay her the allowance under the provisions of the Criminal Procedure Code. The Court had been approached by Ahmed Khan with the plea that he had fulfilled his obligations to his ex-wife in accordance with the Muslim personal law, and he was not bound to maintain her any further. However, the Court ruled that the criminal laws override the personal laws, and they are applicable to all Indian citizens irrespective of their creed.

This judgement sparked a tremendous controversy, which has had serious repercussions for the Indian law and state. Large sections of the Muslim community saw the judgement as an abrogation of their religious-cultural rights by the state. Political pressure on the government and the ruling Congress Party forced the then Prime Minister, Rajiv Gandhi, to enact new parliamentary legislation, called the Muslim Women (Protection of Rights on Divorce) Bill, 1986. The Bill made provisions such that the Criminal Procedure Code would not apply to Muslim women.

The controversy generated by the Shah Bano case and the subsequent Bill is still far from over. It has many dimensions. The dominant themes are community, state, and gender relations. Some people are most concerned about safeguarding the cultural rights and autonomy of religious and other communities. In this case, the cultural autonomy of a religious minority was considered to be at stake. The Muslim community was divided on the issue, but in the prevailing political atmosphere a large majority was opposed to the Supreme Court judgment. This was the reason why Rajiv Gandhi was forced to bring the Bill that would undo the effects of the Court judgement. On the other side, people felt that nothing could override the claims of the state, which was democratically constituted by the entire citizenry, and was concerned with ensuring the protection of rights and the common good of all, in its capacity as the supreme representative institution. The issue was further complicated by the rise of Hindu communalism, and the political ascendance of the Hindu Right. The demand for a uniform civil code was turned into a slogan of the Hindu communal campaign against the Muslim minority.

The complexity of the issue has weighed heavily on the women's movement too. It is not as simple as rising to defend Shah Bano's rights, and women's rights in general. One has to think about the dangers of the current rise of the Hindu Right, and about the apprehensions of the Muslim minority, which increasingly has a sense of being besieged by the aggressive communalism of the Hindu majority. At another level, one has to think about the issue of cultural rights, and about the relationship between community and state. The Court clearly favoured Shah Bano as a woman, but where should society draw a line beyond which the rights of women as individuals can override the rights of a community? Within the feminist movement there have been debates and controversies on all these issues since the case was determined.

In my view, the bottom line is that, in this case, cultural practices prevented the realisation of the rights of Muslim women, including their right to equal citizenship. The need to win elections can lead to politicians being influenced by the cultural sensitivities of a section of the electorate. The result here was that a retrograde step was taken against women's rights by a Prime Minister who had become famous for his pledge to take India into the twenty-first century.

The Bhanwari Devi case

The case of Bhanwari Devi is very well known in India, especially in the women's movement and the NGO sector. A feature film, *Bawandar*, has been made of Bhanwari's story. My account here is based on internal documents of women's organisations that took up the campaign in Bhanwari's support, and on my own familiarity with the case.[5]

On 15 November 1995, the District and Sessions Court of Jaipur, Rajasthan, passed a judgement acquitting five men who had gang-raped Bhanwari Devi. Bhanwari was a *Sathin* (village-level woman worker) in the Women's Development Programme run by the State of Rajasthan. She had joined the programme in 1985, and had become a relentless campaigner against the practice of child marriage. This practice is very common in Rajasthan. Bhanwari had successfully prevented the marriage of the one-year-old daughter of Ram Karan Gujar. Bhanwari and her husband, Mohan, were often harassed and threatened on account of her campaign against this practice; but this time a ghastly 'punishment' was meted out. On 22 September 1992, she was gang-raped by five men. Ram Karan Gujar was one of them.

The reasons given in the judgment for acquitting the accused were remarkable. First, the court rejected the testimony of Bhanwari's husband. A press release supportive of Bhanwari reported: 'The judgment discredits his testimony by stating that "in our society, how can an Indian husband whose role is to protect his wife, stand by and watch his wife be raped?" The fact that there were five offenders who assaulted Mohan (two of who were convicted of simple assault in the same judgment) has been conveniently side-stepped' (NGO press release in support of Bhanwari Devi, 1995). Another argument was even more remarkable: 'According to the judge, the rapists are middle-aged and therefore respectable citizens, whilst rape is "usually committed by teenagers". In addition, the judgment states that, "since the offenders were upper-caste men and included a Brahmin, the rape could not have

taken place, because Bhanwari was from a lower caste"'(ibid.).

Bhanwari's assailants were locally powerful people, while she came from a poor and low-caste family. However, these locally powerful elements could not have counted for much in the macro-level power structure. Though powerful in relation to Bhanwari, they too were relatively poor villagers, who could hardly influence a District Judge. The views expressed in the judgement had their origin in the fact that the Judge had typical patriarchal, caste-bound, and class-bound prejudices. These cultural prejudices overrode the constitutional role and the sense of justice expected of him. This is a clear example of how pre-modern cultural factors can prevail over a modernist constitutional legal structure.

Today, Bhanwari is still seeking justice. Refusing numerous offers of a compromise, she has struggled to bring the case to a higher court. She has found support in the women's organisations and other civil-society organisations, which have helped to transform her into a symbol of women's courage and dedication to the cause of gender justice and emancipation. Ten years later, there are perceptible changes in the atmosphere in some parts of society. On International Women's Day 2003, a women's organisation, Stree Adhikar Sangathan, honoured Bhanwari in a Delhi University auditorium, and hundreds of students, teachers, scholars, and activists gave her a prolonged standing ovation. This is a small indication of the big changes that are taking place, often imperceptibly, on the gender scene in India.

Alinagar killings[6]

On 7 August 2001, a young couple were hanged by their own family members in the village of Alinagar in the Muzaffarnagar district of western Uttar Pradesh. In the cultural atmosphere of this region, choosing one's own partner can be a hazardous thing to do. Marriages are arranged by the family elders. If young people choose their own partners, across castes or communities, their action can easily lead to a murderous end. There have been cases in this region in which the village *panchayat* (village council) has pronounced a death penalty on an erring couple, and they have been executed by hanging from a tree in front of the whole village. There was even an infamous case in which the mother of a young man from a lower caste, who had eloped with a girl from an upper-caste family, was raped by several men on the orders of the village *panchayat*. Criminal cases arising out of these murders and rapes have often not made much progress, as no one will testify in court. The entire community seems to support these cultural norms and practices.

The young woman in this case was Sonu, aged 17, who belonged to a rich Jat[7] family. The young man, Vishal, belonged to a Brahmin family of the same village. They were found together, in a 'compromising position'. The murder was committed in the house of a poor low-caste woman, by the father of the girl and the brother of the boy. After the hanging, the entire village participated in the burning of the bodies, which was hastily done on the same night soon after the murder. No one from the village informed the police. The next day, the police received an anonymous call about the incident and performed a routine check. They found confirmation that the crime had actually taken place. As no one was willing to file a First Information Report (FIR), the police sub-inspector himself lodged the FIR in his own handwriting. Thirteen out of the 16 persons named in the FIR were soon arrested. When a fact-finding team, consisting of four women activists from four different organisations, visited the village, it found that no one had mourned the dead, except perhaps Vishal's mother, who had since moved out of the village. Nothing has happened in the case as yet, which may go on for years. Meanwhile, the village remains united in shielding the murderers, who are seen as having done what honour and tradition demanded.

Concluding remarks

Challenging the cultural practices of a community, let alone of a 'civilisation', is a formidable and enormously complex task. However, changes in culture do occur, even if over long periods of time, and there are famous and heroic examples in history when such changes have been brought about through conscious and planned interventions. Social movements are the best and the most effective mediators of cultural change. As Bryan Turner has pointed out, social movements are 'inevitably movements about the rights of citizenship' (Turner 1986, 92).

This has important implications for the development sector. Social movements are rooted in their own societies. The development sector, on the other hand, has an increasingly global character, as discussed earlier in this article, and it is mostly driven from the North. In the absence of robust and transparent mechanisms for democratic control and supervision over the global organisations, the development interventions of such organisations are likely to be seen as colonial. If the development sector aspires, as it must, to address the issue of harmful cultural practices, it must win popular legitimacy in the societies of the South. This requires innovative and effective partnerships to be created between local social movements and the development sector. This is of crucial importance if conditions are to be created whereby the right to equal citizenship is realised by women in societies like India.

Kanchan Sinha is the North India Programme Manager of Oxfam GB in India. She has a Ph.D. in philosophy and was a university teacher in the early part of her career. She specialises in gender and development. She has been active in the women's movement for the last two decades. ksinha@oxfam.org.uk

Notes

1 'Cultural relativism' can be defined as the belief that it is impossible to formulate uniform criteria of judgement that apply across cultural boundaries. The notions of justice, rights, gender equality, human dignity, and other such concepts would, according to the cultural relativist view, change from one culture to another.

2 See, for example, Kapur and Cossman (1999).

3 See Menon (1999), 'Rights, bodies and the law: rethinking feminist politics of justice', in Menon (ed.) (1999).

4 Literature on the Shah Bano controversy is extensive. See, for example, Hasan (2000), and Palriwala and Agnihotri (1998).

5 See also Human Rights Watch (1999, 176).

6 Information here comes from AALI (2001).

7 This is a landowning middle-level caste that is socially dominant in the north-western region of the country around the national capital, Delhi.

References

AALI (2001) 'Report of the Fact-finding Team', Lucknow: Association for Advocacy and Legal Initiative

Coomaraswamy, R. (2002) 'Integration of the Human Rights of Women and the Gender Perspective: Violence against Women', Report of the Special Rapporteur on Violence against Women, its Causes and Consequences, submitted in accordance with Commission on Human Rights resolution 2001/49, United Nations, E/CN.4/2003/83, 31 January 2002

Dhagamwar, V. (1992) *Law, Power and Justice: The Protection of Personal Rights in the Indian Penal Code*, New Delhi: Sage Publications

Hasan, Z. (2000) 'Uniform civil code and gender justice in India', in P.R. deSouza (ed.) *Contemporary India – Transitions*, New Delhi: Sage Publications

Human Rights Watch (1999) *Broken People: Caste Violence against India's 'Untouchables'*, New York: Human Rights Watch

Kapur, R. and B. Cossman (1999) 'On women, equality and the constitution: through the looking glass of feminism', in N. Menon (ed.) (1999)

Menon, N. (ed.) (1999) *Gender and Politics in India*, New Delhi: Oxford University Press

Palriwala, R. and I. Agnihotri (1998) 'Tradition, the family and the State: politics of the contemporary women's movement', in T.V. Satyamurthy (ed.) *Region, Religion, Caste, Gender and Culture in Contemporary India*, Delhi: Oxford University Press

Turner, B.S. (1986) *Citizenship and Capitalism*, London: Allen and Unwin

Algerian women, citizenship, and the 'Family Code'

Zahia Smail Salhi

Women's struggle for both equality and national liberation are crucial to democracy: if a democratic state is one in which citizens have the right to participate in society and the way it is governed, women must, automatically, be included in the equation. Yet in many so-called democratic states, women lack full citizenship.This article traces Algerian women's struggle for full citizenship after the national liberation struggle ended in 1962. The Algerian Family Code, which became law in 1984, proclaims women to be minors under the law, and defines them as existing only in so far as they are daughters, mothers, or wives. Algerian women are demanding that the government repeal the Family Code; challenging patriarchal values that prevail in Algerian society; and resisting and fighting Islamic fundamentalism.

The rebellion of Algerian women during the national liberation struggle was on two fronts: it was, simultaneously, a rebellion against the colonial occupation of Algeria by France, and against the restrictive attitudes of traditional Algerian society. Women were active agents in the revolution. Their contribution ranged from fighting beside men, planting bombs, and carrying weapons, to nursing the sick and wounded in the *maquis* (fighting fronts), and, above all, keeping the revolution moving forward. The Italian-Algerian film, *The Battle of Algiers* (directed by Pontecorvo in 1965), though rarely screened now, records women's extraordinary courage.

Women's new status as activists during the war not only altered the division of labour between women and men, but also challenged the wider power of patriarchy, threatening to erode its power and privileges. Rejecting their restricted role as mothers, wives, and daughters in the private sphere of the household, women took on active roles in a wide public sphere. Their work was integral to the struggle for national liberation and, therefore, equally important to their own liberation. Yet Algerian women are now trapped between the dictates of an infamous Family Code, which became law in 1984, and the barbarism of Islamic fundamentalists.

Progress on women's rights during the liberation war

The FLN (*Front de Libération Nationale*, or National Liberation Front) had a policy committing it to women's equality, and the policy was put into practice in certain situations during the war. One example was the institution of tribunals before which couples were married on the basis of the partners' mutual consent. Woodhull observes, 'At the time of the Algerian revolution and at the time of independence the emerging nation still held the promise of social equality for women, whose fundamental role in the war had been recognised by the

National Liberation Front', (Woodhull 1993, 10). In the late 1980s, however, this progress seemed to be lost. One woman states: 'Our only regret is the loss of that absolute equality achieved during the revolution. As far as that's concerned, we seem to have moved backwards rather than forwards' (Shaaban 1988, 199).

However, some argue that the beginnings of the backlash against women's rights occurred during the national liberation struggle: 'Our return to the "inside" didn't begin in 1962, but, rather, before independence. Little by little, during the war, the FLN removed us from the real fighting zones and sent us to the borders or overseas. Our role was defined from that moment on. We didn't have any place in the world of the "outside"' (Messaoudi and Schemla 1998, 51).

What is clear is that the majority of Algerian men did not acknowledge the need for women's emancipation. Those who did often saw it as a secondary priority in relation to the endless list of other issues facing the government. Soon after independence, Algerian men cut the strong ties that they had forged with their female compatriots, and denied them their basic civil rights.

An example of this betrayal of women as equals was the way in which many fighters who achieved good social or political positions after independence repudiated their wives, and married girls whose youth reflected positively on their husbands at social events. Buthaina Shaaban reports the testimony of a woman war veteran, who describes this as common practice: 'This was very common. In fact, it was the norm. There were lots of men who married their women comrades in the mountains. Once they came down, however, and got good positions or good jobs in the towns, they divorced their comrades and got married to younger, more presentable, women.' The same woman war veteran related this directly to the betrayal of women's citizenship rights: 'As women, we paid the price from every point of view, and now they won't allow us to put our own laws on the market. I am convinced that all men are aware that women understand things a lot better than they do. That's why they feel inferior to us, and instead of having the courage to face us they try to keep us down. How long it will take us to outwit them, just as we outwitted the French, I don't know. Not very long, I hope' (Shaaban 1988, 200).

The 1976 Constitution

In 1976, the FLN government agreed a new Constitution after a referendum. The Constitution promoted the emancipation of women, and deplored the way in which the old feudal system had restricted their rights. It stated that equality of the sexes and freedom of movement were guaranteed by law. The Constitution acknowledged the role of the Algerian revolution in enabling women to liberate themselves as well as their country, and insisted that the status of women still needed improvement. It emphasised the state's efforts to this end, in granting women their political rights, and exalted the socialist regime adopted by the government as a democratic movement which would promote justice, strive against backward thinking, and change the justice system in women's favour. The Constitution held Islam to be a liberating power, considering women to be equal to men.

Nevertheless, the text of the Constitution stated that women must lead this battle for their emancipation: 'It is woman herself who must ultimately remain the best defender of her own rights and dignity through her deportment and qualities as well as a relentless struggle against prejudice, injustice, and humiliation… As for the state, it has already recognised woman's political rights, and is committed to her education and inevitable social advancement' (Lazreg, cited in Joseph 2000, 63).

After the death of the first post-Revolution head of state, President Boumedienne, in 1978, Chadli Bendjedid was named

President of Algeria by the Islamo-ba'thist clan.[1] 'The objective of this clan, beyond ensuring that Algerian assets continued to yield a profit to their benefit, was to place the country under the law of *charia* [sic]. To succeed, they had to launch a simultaneous attack on the three pillars on which they planned to base that project: women, education, and the justice system' (Messaoudi and Schemla 1998, 48). Although, until then, clan members were only a minority in Algeria's single party, they soon won over the socialist modernists.

Restrictions on women's citizenship rights

In 1980, the Constitutional commitment to freedom of movement was broken by a ministerial order prohibiting women from travelling unaccompanied by a male relative. This decision became public knowledge when a group of women, who were enrolled in universities abroad, were stopped at the airport and prevented from travelling to join their universities. This demonstrated that women's citizenship was perceived as a privilege that the state could withdraw at any time. Although the women attempted to trigger a public scandal about this infringement of their civil rights, the echoes of the event were only timidly reported in the Algerian daily *El-Moujahid* and the weekly *Algérie Actualités*. A group of women, including many university students, signed a long petition and asked to meet the Minister of the Interior. On 8 March 1980, a huge demonstration was organised to mark International Women's Day, and demand that the order hampering women's freedom of movement be abolished. In the end, Chadli's government retreated: the ministerial order was cancelled (Messaoudi and Schemla 1998, 49).

The following year, Chadli's government prepared a pilot study of a proposed new Family Code. The newspapers reported that the Code was an attempt to placate a growing tendency towards Islamic fundamentalism and, as such, threatened women's rights and privileges as fully enfranchised citizens.

Outraged, a hundred feminist activists in Algiers staged a sit-in in the offices of the UNFA (*Union Nationale des Femmes Algériennes*, or National Union of Algerian Women), a state organisation, established soon after independence in 1962, and affiliated to the FLN. The women demanded to see the classified text of the pilot study. The UNFA replied that Algerian women were not aware of their rights and had, therefore, nothing to discuss (Messaoudi and Schemla 1998). If Algerian women were not aware of their rights, as claimed, independent feminists asserted that this was because the UNFA had not played the vital role of promoting women's interests after independence. Rather, the women of the UNFA were more concerned with international political issues, and distanced themselves from the real dilemmas of the women of Algeria, whom they were supposed to represent.

The outcome was a complete rupture between the UNFA and feminists outside, who were determined to continue the fight for the rights of Algerian women. On 28 October 1981, women demonstrated in the streets, expressing their wrath at the government's decision to debate the Family Code in secret. Two weeks later, on 16 November 1981, 500 women gathered in front of the National Assembly as it met for a plenary session. One of them, Khalida Messaoudi, testified later: 'We had gathered more than ten thousand signatures of support from all over Algeria. Along with two friends, I marched into the assembly chambers. Rabah Bitat, the assembly president, was obliged to adjourn the session. The assembly leaders skilfully manipulated the situation: we were given four days to make propositions for amending the text. The movement became divided at that point: there were those who wanted to accept the deal, and those who rejected it' (Messaoudi and Schemla 1998, 49).

The ultimate outcome was that the text went ahead unchanged.

The date 23 December 1981 is considered an important day in the history of the secular feminist movement in Algeria. That day, women war veterans joined the young feminist activists and voiced their rejection of the government's introduction of the Family Code. This was seen as a betrayal of what they had fought for. Young and old gathered in front of the main post office in Algiers. The demonstrators carried slogans reading, 'No to Silence, Yes to Democracy!' and 'No to the betrayal of the ideals of November 1, 1954!'. Despite this solidarity, and intensified protests, the women's groups failed to stop the Family Code from passing into law in June 1984.

The Family Code and women's rights

Marnia Lazreg states, 'Family law has often codified the ownership of wives and children by fathers/husbands' (Lazreg, cited in Joseph 2000, 21). The Family Code of 1984 makes it a legal duty for Algerian women to obey their husbands, and respect and serve them, their parents, and relatives (Article 39). It institutionalised polygamy and made it the right of men to take up to four wives (Article 8). Women cannot arrange their own marriage contracts unless represented by a matrimonial guardian (Article 11), and they have no right to apply for divorce. While a man needs only to desire a divorce to get one, it is made a most difficult, if not impossible, thing to be obtained by women. Women may obtain divorce only by submitting to the practice of *kho'a*, (Article 54) 'which allows women to divorce on the condition that they give up any claim to alimony. Khol'a [sic] is the problematic ransom that women must pay for their freedom, just like slaves' (Messaoudi and Schemla 1998, 53). The Family Code assigns the role of procreator to women, making it a legal duty for them to breastfeed their children and care for them until adulthood (Article 48), although they are not responsible for children's education (Article 63). Yet women have no right to pass their name, nationality, or religion to their children, and if they marry a foreigner they are crossed out of the country's registration books altogether.

The consequences of divorce are dramatic for both women and children: wives and mothers have no right to the family home, since this is automatically awarded to the husband. Moreover, the state does nothing to provide housing or financial support for divorced mothers. Consequently, in the absence of assistance from their parents, divorced women often find themselves on the streets with their children. As for custody of the children after divorce, the mother cannot become the carer of her children until adulthood unless their father agrees to it. The mother can never become the tutor of her children, and the father's consent and permission are needed for the most basic needs of the child, including registering him or her at school, and even approving the child's participation in school activities (Articles 52, 62, 65). On the other hand, the law does not punish the father if he decides not to provide for his children.

In the 19 years since the Family Code came into force, Algeria has seen increasing levels of homelessness among women and children. Thousands of mothers wander the streets with their children; others sell their labour as domestic servants at very cheap rates. The streets of Algeria's major cities are the homes of many desperate divorced women. Some of them have found shelter in the slums; others have sought refuge in the hostels run by the organisation SOS Women in Distress. However, according to newspaper reports, this organisation is unable to cope with the large number of requests it receives every day, because of its lack of financial backing.

Although the authors of this Code claim it to be merely based on the teachings of *Shari'a* law, it is clear from its text that its roots emanate from a tradition of patriarchy and misogyny in Algeria, which was taken up in a particular way in the post-colonial era. A clear example comes in Article 38. The content of this article relates to married women's rights in wedlock: a wife has the right to visit her parents, and they the right to visit her according to local custom. In post-colonial Algeria, women were seen (as in the pre-revolutionary period) as the repositories of men's honour; as guardians of the traditional values which had been disrupted and devalued by the colonial presence. They were also symbols that represented the conflicts inherent in the new historical situation faced by post-colonial Algeria. Hence, the Family Code placed limits on women's mobility.

Some articles in the Family Code reflect the economic crisis in Algeria in the mid-1980s. An example is Article 52, which relates to the family home in case of divorce. The article states clearly that the husband may allow his wife and children to live in the family home if he possesses more than one house, which is a rarity in a country where housing shortages are a major problem. Also, this leaves it up to the man to decide to be generous or not. Once again women are dependent on male whims.

In her book, *Women and Islam*, Fatima Mernissi states: 'If women's rights are a problem for some modern Muslim men, it is neither because of the Koran [sic] nor the prophet, nor the Islamic tradition, but simply because those rights conflict with the interests of a male elite. The elite faction is trying to convince us that their egotistic, highly subjective, and mediocre view of culture and society has a sacred basis' (Mernissi 1991, ix).

Women's response to the Family Code

Determined to challenge the Family Code, the women of Algeria embarked on a long, painful, and lonely battle. Khalida Messaoudi asserts: 'Men were painfully absent from our struggle. This reinforced my conviction that Algerian women could expect salvation only from themselves' (Messaoudi and Schemla 1998, 56). Since 1984, war veterans and younger feminists have joined together to protest ceaselessly against a piece of legislation that proclaims men to be superior to women and codifies women's subordination.

After many disappointments, the women of Algeria had come to understand that no one else would help them seek emancipation. They knew that they would have to build their own movement, to fight the violation of women's human rights. Khalida Messaoudi testifies: 'I had the feeling that the deepest injustice had been perpetuated. We had been had, totally had, and we could do nothing but bang our heads against the wall, because we knew that this text was going to structure the entire society from that point on. For me, the whole business had really opened my eyes: The traitor in this story was the Algerian state' (Messaoudi and Schemla 1998, 55).

Unrest and political reform

Nearly two decades after the imposition of the Family Code, political reforms have since occurred in Algeria in response to popular protest. However, the Family Code remains.

On 5 October 1988, young people took to the streets, calling for an end to the system's oppression and corruption, and demanding dignity and justice. The same day, groups consisting mainly of high-school students and unemployed young people attacked everything that represented the state and the FLN, which was now synonymous with corruption, chaos, and the misuse of public funds. The economic reforms introduced by President Chadli Ben Djedid in the 1980s had failed, creating an anarchic situation as unemployment increased, mainly among the young people who made up 70 per cent of the Algerian population. There were also shortages of all sorts. Among the political elite, tension was growing between those who continued to believe in central planning and those who wanted to liberalise the economy.

The October riots were also an explosion of life that had been repressed for too long. The youths' main objective was to destroy the old system and build a new society which would release the country's unused human potential. They danced and celebrated in the streets of Algiers. Their joy was short-lived, however, as they faced fierce repression soon afterwards. Thousands of arrests were made, and most of the detainees were tortured, while some of them were actually shot by the army: 'Doctors estimated that five hundred people were killed and thousands wounded' (Messaoudi and Schemla 1998, 85).

The youth movement triggered protests and demands for change from many other groups. Seventy Algerian journalists published a declaration in which they denounced the ban on reporting, and condemned the restrictions that were imposed on freedom of speech. They also denounced the violence, torture, and arbitrary arrests used by the state. In short, the whole political system was coming under sustained attack. The Algerian League for Human Rights denounced the practice of torture, while the doctors who saw the results of torture, and the merciless repressive measures undertaken by government forces, became the principal driving force behind the creation of the National Committee Against Torture. They were joined by other groups and organisations, among them militant women's groups, who expressed their full support for the youth movement, and called for the recognition of democratic liberties.

While all sectors of opposition condemned torture, the Islamists maintained silence on the issue. Instead, Ali Benhadj, a high-school teacher, and Abassi Madani, a university professor, issued an anonymous call for a huge demonstration in Algiers. This event was used to hijack the youth movement, using populist rhetoric to express outright hatred of the regime.

In order to save his government, Chadli Ben Djedid gave promises of political reforms, which he launched in November of the same year. A new Constitution was drafted and approved in February 1989. This guaranteed Algerian citizens freedom of expression, association, and assembly (Article 39). It also recognised the right of the citizens to create political associations, meaning political parties (Article 40): 'This amendment allowed for the establishment of a multi-party system, thus terminating, at least theoretically, the FLN's monopoly and making it a *parti comme les autres*' (Zoubir 1993, 90).

Subsequently, a law on political associations was issued. Although it prohibits the foundation of parties set up exclusively to campaign on religious, linguistic, or regionalist issues, several parties that should have been banned under this law were recognised by the government. The best example is the recognition of the Islamic Salvation Front (FIS), whose leaders never supported democracy. Indeed, they asserted that once in power they would implement the *Shari'a* law, which they presented as the solution to every question. They unequivocally declared that they would repeal the republic's constitution and ban secular political parties. 'Ali Benhadj repeated *ad infinitum* that democracy was incompatible with Islam and was *kufr* [blasphemy] because it placed the power of the people over God's power over the people' (Al-Ahnaf et al 1991, 87).

Continuing the struggle for repeal of the Family Code

Despite these tremendous changes on a political level, the Family Code remained unchanged, and there was no question of repealing it. The Islamists argued that *Shari'a* law should be applied throughout society, and called for stricter measures with regard to the treatment of women. Feminist groups and organisations became alarmed, and were particularly worried by the populist misogynous propaganda that the FIS had started to direct at young people. For example, young men were encouraged to believe that they were unemployed because women had taken their jobs. The fundamentalists argued that housework is more suited to female biology and psychology than professional work; that rates of mortality and morbidity are actually higher among employed women than among women who stay at home; that employed women are less moral; and that female employment causes male unemployment.

Although women's organisations have now been legally recognised, and have gained access to a wider audience, thanks to the liberalisation of the media, Islamic fundamentalists continue to pose a threat to activists, first intimidating women's groups and later issuing death threats against their leaders. An example is Khalida Messaoudi, whose life became a daily battle to save her own skin. She has described how, after she received several anonymous death threats over the phone, matters quickly spiralled out of control as verbal attacks were made on her during prayers in mosques associated with the FIS: 'Over the loudspeakers, whose monotonous echoes penetrate into the very centre of the surrounding houses, *imams* (priests) would hurl curses at me, describe me as "a woman of delinquent morals" and a "danger to the morality of women", and warn those women who might be tempted to follow my example' (Messaoudi and Schemla 1998, 87).

In 1992, the Islamic fundamentalists began their violent terrorist campaign to enforce strict observance of *Shari'a* law as it affects women. They demanded that women be forced to wear the veil, and issued death threats against feminist leaders who claimed the most basic civil rights for women in a misogynous culture. Harassment has been relentless and unbearable, particularly for women who live alone or who refuse to wear the veil in the workplace.

For example, as early as June 1989, a fundamentalist gang set fire to the house of a woman from Ouargla, a city in southern Algeria. The sole reason for this act was the fact that she lived alone with her seven children. The fundamentalists claimed that she was a whore. As such, she posed a threat to the health of the community and was a source of discord. One of her children burned to death in the attack. During the same summer, acid was thrown at women on beaches and other public places for publicly exposing parts of their bodies. A nurse was burned by her fundamentalist brother because she was working with men in hospital. An athlete, Hassiba Boulmerka, was declared a shameless renegade in the nation's mosques because she ran 'half naked' in the full gaze of world publicity. She was subject to these attacks after she wore the regulation running shorts and vest when she won the 1500-metres race at the World Athletics Championships in 1991, as only the second Arab woman ever to receive a sporting title of such prestige. Her remarkable performance was, indeed, a source of pride to all Arab women, and Algerian women in particular.

In their tracts FIS members insisted on the importance of women returning to Islam; this was partly because women are regarded by the fundamentalists as symbols and repositories of religious, national, and cultural identity. FIS tracts and leaflets made clear the role attributed to women by Islam: 'Mother, sister, wife, as your father, brother, husband, I would like your beauty to be my wealth, for I cannot live without you. I see the with jealousy when I see you working as a secretary for a human fox, who asked for your photo before he hired you. I don't want you to be a work tool, or a scapegoat for those who seek to destroy Islamic morals... I don't want you to use the Jewish word "emancipation" to attack the Islamic values of your ancestors and make the feminist organisation happy' (quoted in Messaoudi and Schemla 1998, 92). The discourse of the FIS regarding women is not much different from that of the FLN. Both parties ignore the enormous socio-economic changes that have happened in Algeria in recent years. Women have suffered just as much as men from the unprecedented economic crisis of the 1980s. Furthermore, not all women 'enjoy' male protection: fewer and fewer families are able to take in divorced women and their children.

The 1990s have been known as a decade of terrorist violence, but this decade also saw flourishing women's movements in Algeria. They are now voicing their bitterness, concerns, and determination to resist the misogyny so prevalent in the country, using a variety of channels. Algeria has heard women's angry voices at demonstrations in the streets of major cities, the voices of female political leaders in Parliament and various political groupings, and the voices of Algerian women writers using a variety of literary forms. All these female voices condemn and unmask the barbarity and the misogyny of the fundamentalists. Women were the first to demonstrate bluntly against Islamic terrorism and its anti-democratic approach. They reminded the world of the 100,000 Algerian victims massacred during the 1990s, out of which women and children account for 80 per cent of the fatalities. They also called for an end to Algerian society's silence over the crime of systematic rape.

Fearless of the consequences, women rape survivors have courageously testified to the media about the hideous act of gang rape, to which many women were subjected. On a regular basis, newspapers have reported atrocities in which terrorists abduct women at random, rape them, make them wash and cook for them, and finally kill them or dismiss them. For example, on 11 March 2000, *El Watan* reported on the scandal of the '5,000 victims people want to hide'. Twelve-year-old Nora was 'kidnapped from her school gates, held, raped repeatedly, and discovered by the security forces six months later, no longer in her right mind and more than three months pregnant' (CMF MENA 2000, 27). When Nora requested to be reunited with her parents, her father disowned her, insisting that his daughter was killed.

Because Algerian families feel shamed by the rape of a female relative, they condemn the survivors of rape to even more suffering, as they end up homeless or (in the best of cases) in charity hostels. The silence imposed on the subject of rape in Algeria is not only the work of individual families, but also that of the government, which fails to condemn organised rape as a crime against humanity, and fails to acknowledge that its victims are victims of torture, in need of support and counselling.

The new government: a commitment to social justice

The end of the 1990s brought a radical change in Algerian politics, Abdul Aziz Bouteflika was elected the new President of the country, promising to promote social justice and, more importantly, to put an end to terrorist violence. The government announced an amnesty in July 1999, and vast numbers of terrorists surrendered, apparently bringing the violence to a halt. Once again women supported the new President and voted massively for his programme; nevertheless, whenever asked about the issue of women in Algeria, he tactfully replied that they made up the majority of the Algerian population. Happy to see terrorist violence coming to a halt, women believed in the good faith of President Abdul Aziz Bouteflika, and eminent feminists like Khalida Messaoudi gave him their full support and became part of his team.

The new government has made major compromises with the Islamist terrorist groups, yet it has so far not acknowledged women's ordeal under the dictates of the inequitable Family Code. After a year in office, the President was questioned by an Algerian female journalist during a press conference in Canada regarding the repealing of the code. He first reprimanded her for daring to ask the question. He told her that the time had not yet come for such a move; Algerian women must wait for mentalities to become ready to accept the change. To add insult to injury, he told the journalist that she was pretty, and should therefore not be aggressive.

The government's second priority is to bring about economic stability to the country. One wonders how a nation can hope to achieve such a goal, with 52 per cent of its population living as minors, and being denied their basic civil rights.

Zahia Smail Salhi is Senior Lecturer in the Department of Arabic and Middle Eastern Studies, and a member of the executive committee of the Centre for Gender Studies at Leeds University, UK. She works on issues of gender and development, women and Islam, and also on the representation of Arab women in literature and the media. Address: Department of Arabic, University of Leeds, LS2 9JT, UK. LLCZS@leeds.ac.uk

Notes

1 In the Algerian army, there are two tendencies; one secular, often French-educated, and the other non-secular, often educated in the Arab East, and believing and insisting on the Arabic and Islamic identity of the country. This tendency calls for the promotion of Arabic as the only official language, and Islam as the religion of the state.

References

Al-Ahnaf, M., B. Botiveau, and F. Frégosi (2001) *L'Algérie par ses Islamistes*, Paris: Karthala

CMF MENA (2000) 'Women's Rights and the Arab Media', London: Centre for Media Freedom Middle East and North Africa

Joseph, S. (ed.) (2000) *Gender and Citizenship in the Middle East*, Syracuse: University Press

Mernissi, F. (1991) *Women and Islam: An Historical and Theological Enquiry*, Oxford: Blackwell

Messaoudi, K. and E. Schemla (1998) *Unbowed: An Algerian Woman Confronts Islamic Fundamentalism*, Pennsylvania: University of Pennsylvania Press

République Algérienne Démocratique et Populaire, Ministère de la Justice (1993) *Le Code de la famille (The Family Code)* Algiers: OPU

Shaaban B. (1998) *Both Right and Left Handed: Arab Women Talk about their Lives*, London: Women's Press

Woodhull, W. (1993) *Transfiguration of the Maghreb*, Minneapolis and London: University of Minnesota Press

Zoubir, Y.H. (1993) 'The painful transition from authoritarianism in Algeria', *Arab Studies Quarterly* 15(3): 83-110

New forms of citizenship:
democracy, family, and community in Rio de Janeiro, Brazil

Joanna S. Wheeler[1]

In the context of macro-level political and economic changes, how do poor women and men living in Rio de Janeiro understand the idea of citizenship? Is it relevant to their daily lives? Because the poor have not reaped the rewards of macro-economic reforms and do not have confidence in the effectiveness of formal democratic participation, they have developed new ways of understanding citizenship. These have evolved in response to needs dictated by family, community, and gender relations, helping people to obtain access to the city's resources on a daily basis. Ultimately, citizenship means participation with dignity in the city's life.

Over the past 15 years, significant political and economic changes in Brazil have made a dramatic impact on women and men in poverty. The country moved from military dictatorship to formal democracy in 1988 and adopted a broad-reaching constitution, encoding numerous rights. In a plebiscite[2] held in 1993, 66 per cent of Brazilians confirmed that they wanted to maintain some form of democracy. Economically, the neo-liberal reforms of the Cardoso administration (1992-2000) have replaced the hyperinflation of the 1980s, and the military regime's subsidies designed to promote industrialisation through import substitution.[3]

Despite these changes, people in poverty remain excluded in Rio de Janeiro, on multiple levels: socially, politically, economically, spatially, and in terms of stigma and discrimination. In the *favelas* (illegal land occupations) and housing projects of Rio de Janeiro, the number of urban poor continues to grow; they now comprise 40 per cent of the city's population (UNDP 2001). Economic

participation in the city has become increasingly informal under neo-liberal reform: more than 40 per cent of the population is now employed outside the formal sector (UNDP 2000).

There has been an accompanying informalisation of political activity, as drug-related violence has further eroded the link between poor communities and formal democratic mechanisms. The power of the drug mafias over poor communities in Rio de Janeiro has also eroded the once strong base of residents' associations that represented a more politically united block in the 1980s. Drug traffickers are known as the *poder paralelo* (parallel power), because they control *favelas* and housing projects as if they were independent states, exercising all the powers of an autocratic government over the residents.

Growing financial pressures on families due to neo-liberal reforms have forced more of the women of Rio de Janeiro to participate in the market economy (Bulbeck 1998, 99). In poor families, women's contributions now make up 38 per cent of the family's income (UNECLAC 1997). The pressures of acting as a 'market citizen' do not fit easily with the traditional gender roles for women as mothers and wives. Women's work at home has increased, because neo-liberal reforms have resulted in the erosion of government-sponsored safety nets. As the state withdraws from providing social services, the family and social networks must fill in the gap. Despite women's additional workload, there has been no change in the distribution of household responsibilities. Women are still responsible for the vast majority of child care, cleaning, shopping, and provision of education and health care for the family. This problem is exacerbated in the case of single-mother households, whose number is dramatically on the rise in Brazil. Single mothers now head one in four households in Brazil (up from one in six in 1991), and earn an average US$246 per month, in comparison with men's average of US$344 per month (*Journal do Brasil*, 8 March 2002, 18). Poor women have responded to this tension between their roles in income generation and family care by linking their political participation and income generation directly to family needs.

The following sections will explore these issues in more depth. I draw on my findings from research conducted between September 2001 and March 2002 in Rio de Janeiro, including more than 40 open-ended interviews. The primary source of the research is the interviews conducted with women and men in six extended families from low-income communities (interviews with three to four members of the same family from three generations). These interviews incorporated families from *favelas*, families from housing projects, and families from the working-class suburbs. I also conducted interviews with key community leaders, workers in the non-profit sector, and members of the government.

'Privatisation of citizenship'

National political discourse on democracy and individual rights is very distant from daily struggles for survival. My respondents consistently identified their participation in their own communities – not specific rights or Brazilian national identity – as the core feature of citizenship. Among my respondents, ideas of citizenship seem to have changed through the generations, from a focus on formal political participation to an emphasis on families in low-income communities addressing the serious problems facing residents on a daily basis. These problems include violence, lack of infrastructure, poverty, and inadequate housing and education.

No participant in the research defined citizenship as meaning an individual's entitlement to claim particular rights from a Brazilian state. This is an especially surprising result, given that Brazil passed through a very public process of debating and ratifying a new constitution in 1988, which gave extensive individual rights and privileges to all citizens, such as the right to health care, education, and labour protections. Both the concept of individual rights, and formal democratic practices, (such as signing petitions, joining political parties, and participating in commissions), have been heavily promoted by the state and also by international non-government organisations (NGOs). It is also surprising since, partly due to Brazil's history of populist regimes enforcing a national identity, 'Brazilian-ness' is believed to be widely valued as a category of identity (Davis 1999; Marx 1998; Machado 1980).

It appears that, while democracy and democratic impulses are important to poor women and men in Rio de Janeiro's *favelas*, they have redefined democratic practice in terms of their own values and beliefs, moving away from the national discourse of individual rights-based democratic practices. Instead, they focus on practices that ensure the survival and well-being of their own families and community. Citizenship is expressed through specific forms of community participation, which provide essential resources and services for the family.

Several factors contribute to the distance between formal democratic mechanisms and the daily lives of poor women and men. Very few respondents could identify any major difference in their lives under dictatorship and democracy, meaning that formal democratic reforms have not dramatically affected their everyday lives. One participant claimed, 'I much prefer a legitimate dictatorship to a false democracy. What we have is a false democracy.' In particular, poor women consistently identified lack of access to urban services, jobs, adequate housing, education, and health care as evidence that they did not in fact live in a democracy – or at least that formal democracy had no meaning for them. They characterised their participation in family, community, and city life as the most meaningful aspect of their political participation.[4]

Participants from one housing project ringed by *favelas* identified the construction of a community centre as their most important form of political participation.[5] One man, living with his wife and two small children in a nearby housing project, who had committed considerable time and energy to community improvements, initiated this project. Although he has a job at the local university as a security guard, he has negotiated extended leave to carry out community development projects of his own design. Because the drug traffickers have taken control of the community where he lives, including control of the local political structure, he has developed a form of activism which carefully negotiates between the traffickers, other established local activists, and his own family's well-being. He has claimed a piece of land in one of the *favelas* to construct a centre to address

the problems that he recognises in his community: lack of education and access to the job market, and poor infrastructure. The future centre will perform a wealth of functions: it will house a community association board, a recycling centre, language training, information-technology training, and a children's choir.

Over the past six years, friends and family members have contributed labour and money to start construction on the centre. Every day, the man who began the work walks through the community to see who has time to help for a few hours. Every day, children collect empty plastic bottles for the community centre's future recycling programme. Hundreds of bottles are stacked in one corner of the construction site. After six years, the first floor has yet to be completed. This is because, when there is no money or time, the project stops until circumstances improve, and the centre receives no support from government or NGOs. The instigator explained that 'the community centre is being built one bag of cement at a time – but it will be built'. He plans to name the centre after his daughter, reasoning that building it has 'taken the food out of her mouth, but it will make her life better'.

Most people involved in the construction had little or no interest in citywide or statewide politics. They consistently identified this community work as important to their own families, and they did not believe that the city government could ever do anything to address the problems in their community. At the community level, democratic impulses[6] in *favelas* are transformed into creative projects to improve specific aspects of the community. The major motivation for these projects, according to the participants in the study, was to build a better life for their children or their families.

'Qualified participation' in the market and formal politics

In the interviews that I conducted with men and women in *favelas*, participants consistently emphasised that their participation in their community and their city was more important than formal political participation, such as voting.

The people whom I interviewed, including self-identified community activists, saw democratic practice as being about participation in a just society, rather than being about formal political issues, such as open and fair elections and individual rights. For the poor, the evidence that society is not intrinsically just and fair is all around them, in the form of police raids, overcrowded buses, inadequate schools, and crumbling and overcrowded health clinics. In *favelas*, voting and formal political participation in Brazil's institutional democracy was seen as relatively unimportant. Democracy has been reclaimed and redefined to mean participation and contribution to family, community, and city life. In response to a question about political participation, one veteran community activist told me: 'I don't feel diminished because I live in a *favela* – each of us has tried to improve our own lives. All the intellectuals who came here, poor things – they never really understood anything because the changes you can make depend on the opportunities you take. [Governments] change and time passes and goes by, but who knows – tomorrow I might manage to do something else [to help the community].'

Several factors have contributed to the shift away from formal political and economic participation towards activity that focuses on the needs of family and community. More than 90 per cent of the participants interviewed said they did not trust the national government. This distrust of the formal political structure goes deeper than any particular administration. One

poor black woman, who lives in a city housing project, said: 'Brazil would be better off with a dictatorship. At least then things were working.' Another poor elderly woman from the suburbs could only identify 'more buses' as the major difference in her life between dictatorship and democracy.

In the 1993 plebiscite mentioned earlier, only 66 per cent voted to maintain democracy (either as presidential or parliamentary), while 11 per cent voted for a monarchy, and an additional 33 per cent voted for 'other form of government'.[7] Several participants voted against democracy for Brazil. One woman explained that she voted for the monarchy, because she did not believe that the form of government would make any difference in her life, and 'a king or queen sounds more interesting than a president.' The refusal of several participants to take such a vote seriously, demonstrated by their choice of the highly improbable monarchy, is a symptom of deep mistrust and disinterest in macro-level politics. In total, 44 per cent of the population voted *against* democracy, which is a significant number, given the length of the military dictatorship.

Governance in Rio de Janeiro: violence and poder paralelo

The violence in Rio de Janeiro, while endemic, is not homogeneous. It is, to use Holston and Appadurai's phrase, 'a city-specific violence of citizenship', meaning that it affects specific places and persons differently (Holston and Appadurai 1999, 16). The level of violence in some parts of the city peaked at 80 homicides per 100,000 people (equivalent to the levels of violence in Colombia and South Africa). From 1995 to 2000, the levels of violence declined somewhat (UNDP 2001), but in the past year there has been a significant resurgence, culminating in the bombing of city government buildings, bus burnings, and army occupation of the streets during the 2003 Carnival.[8] The highest rates of violence are in *favelas* and poor neighbourhoods

40

inhabited by Afro-Brazilians (Zona Oeste and Zona Norte) (UNDP 2001). In these areas, the violence takes the form of state-sponsored raids and battles with drug mafias (in 2001 more than 900 civilians were killed by the police in Rio de Janeiro), and wars between competing factions and mafias of the drug trade (UNDP 2001).

Violence related to drug trafficking, and the invasive power of drug mafias over poor communities in Rio de Janeiro, means that national democratic citizenship has little meaning for the participants in this research. The extremely high levels of violence dramatically affect the daily lives of the residents. It is unsafe to use public spaces like streets, bus stops, and plazas after dark, and increasingly during the day. In one housing project involved in the study, a faction of traffickers took control of the local school, while another took control of the local day-care nursery, and the children were unable to attend for more than a month, for fear of being caught in the crossfire between the warring groups.

The overall result is that formal political rights become ever less relevant for the poor: 'Democratic rights are compromised by other power circuits [including the military police, and the drug and gambling mafias] that obliterate the public dimension of citizenship, re-establishing violence and arbitrary power in the sphere of private relations, class, gender and ethnicity, thereby rendering the state increasingly ineffective…'(Paoli and Telles 1998, 65).

Recasting citizenship through the family

As highlighted earlier, residents in Rio de Janeiro's *favelas* face exclusion from the city, a problem which is exacerbated by extremely poor schools, drug-related violence, and poor infrastructure. Almost every respondent considered participation in the market through paid employment, both formal and informal, to be essential. The ideals of neo-liberalism – that is, the 'market logic' of efficiency, competitiveness, and individualism – have interacted in unexpected ways

with notions of citizenship in *favelas*. These economic ideals have been widely discussed in public, and heavily promoted by the state. For example, Rio de Janeiro's city government has set up numerous micro-credit and funding programmes.

The market, and certain aspects of market-driven logic, have become prevalent in *favelas*, but *favela* residents have adapted market practices to the needs of their own family and community structures. The family has become the point of articulation between the market and individuals. That is to say, the participants in this study on the whole did not approach the market as individuals, but rather as members of families. Getting a job, credit, and obtaining access to education and health care were mediated by family needs and relationships. Certain aspects of 'market logic' are promoted, while others are rejected.

For example, one woman to whom I spoke lives with her husband and son in a house built on the family's property, together with more than 40 members of her extended family. The land was inherited from her great-grandfather, who emigrated from Portugal. Although her salary as a housekeeper in the city is essential income for the family, she commutes nearly five hours a day to the city centre, in order to continue to live with her family. Several employers have offered her accommodation in the city during the week, so that she can avoid this lengthy and costly commute, but she refuses to move away from her family. She uses her salary to pay for daily household expenses, while her husband's salary goes towards bills. When she has extra money, she transfers her son from state-funded to private school.

While my respondent could save a considerable amount by living in Rio and avoiding transportation costs, she refuses to do this. When she became seriously ill, her mother and sister (also housekeepers in the city centre) filled in at her jobs, so that she would not lose them. Her other sister stays at home and provides child care for the extended family, and also does the washing and cleaning. Although she could make more money if she were to get a job outside the home, she and her sisters believe it is more important for her to provide child care and laundry services for the family. Together, these women are participating in the market to secure jobs, health care, child care, and education for their children. However, while they participate in the market, and make rational economic decisions, paid work is only one element in their livelihood strategy as members of a family. The family works together to respond to crisis and uncertainty, fulfilling market demand for cheap day-labour in the city, but using the connections of family members to guarantee other benefits.

The need for women to integrate themselves into the market has affected family structures, and the gendered division of labour. Increasing numbers of women travel long distances for work, while men are more likely to find work nearer to the home (UNDP 2000). Women with little formal education are most likely to work in the informal service sector – for example, as housekeepers, cooks, or nannies – and must travel from the low-income communities ringing the city into more wealthy areas closer to the city centre. Men from low-income communities, on the other hand, often find work in civil construction, factories, or other manual work – which is often much closer to low-income areas of the city. Since women are still responsible for household tasks, this puts an increasing strain on them to fulfil their work obligations. As a result, men are forced to take a larger role in the home. Women's entry into the labour market has also increased their control over family finances, and women often opt to keep their children in school for longer than would have been possible if they were not working.

Citizenship and dignity

The final piece in this narrative of citizenship from poor communities in Rio de Janeiro is the issue of dignity in everyday life. Dignity was the most important aspect of citizenship identified by 74 per cent of the participants of the study. Dignity was strongly associated with their daily attempts to secure education, health care, urban services, and housing from the city authorities. Most participants cited a lack of dignity as proof that they were, in fact, not really citizens at all. One woman said: 'Dignity is everything for a citizen – and we have no dignity. We are treated like cattle in the clinics, on the buses, and in the shops. Only in rich neighbourhoods are people treated with dignity.'

To illustrate what they meant, the participants in this study most frequently referred to their daily experiences of life in the city – especially lack of access to public services including health care, education, urban services, and public housing. Meaningful citizenship cannot exist without dignity. For the participants in this study, it was not poverty or lack of rights that robbed them of dignity. Rather, the difference between dignity and exclusion hinged on their overall experience of survival, with its conflicts and triumphs.

Dignity for the poor, in terms of daily life, meant *dignified* access to public services – facilitated or blocked by women's and men's everyday interactions with the health-care and education systems, urban services, and housing. While access to these public services may be guaranteed by Brazil's constitution as a right, it is the nature of that access that is most important to the poor. The erosion of health, education, housing, and urban services over the past 30 years has compromised the dignity of the poor in everyday life. The participants in this study identified dignified access to these services as the most important characteristics of citizenship, and also the biggest lack in terms of their citizenship.

Public services in Rio de Janeiro: the case of public health care

It is the challenge of regular access to public services, such as the health-care system, that erodes the dignity of the poor in Rio de Janeiro, and it is dignity that they place at the centre of their conception of citizenship. While access may be limited and services poor, it is the nature of such access that most affects participants' daily lives.

The end of the dictatorship coincided with a marked disintegration of many public services, because the new democratic government did not have the funds to make up for 15 years of under-investment and neglect. The neo-liberal reforms over the past eight years have further diminished the resources available for public services. The result is minimal public education and health-care systems, which have been abandoned by anyone with enough money to afford private education or health services.

The public health-care system (*Sistema Único de Saúde Brasiliera*), which is supported by a heavy tax paid by employers, is woefully inadequate. Public hospitals do not have the resources to provide basic care. Currently 40 per cent of the total population in Rio de Janeiro has resorted to private health care (UNDP 2001). The most readily available form of health service for poor women is pre-natal care. Nonetheless, Brazil has the highest mortality rate among pregnant women in Latin America. The United Nations estimates that 200 women die in childbirth for every 100,000 children born (UNECLAC 1997). For all other types of health service, from family planning to treatment for hypertension, one has to wait for months or even years for appointments. In order to be seen by a doctor in a public hospital, the queue starts to form at three o'clock in the morning, to get a ticket to enter the waiting list for an appointment. Several participants in my research reported having travelled for three hours across the entire city with their children, to go to a public hospital that was rumoured to a have better paediatric service. The participants in this study went to great lengths to gain access to private health care and education. Most frequently, this meant women working in domestic-service jobs for the middle classes, and using their employers to gain access to private health care and better education.

The daily struggle of the poor with the public health-care system most clearly demonstrates how lack of dignified access to public services affects their lives. Despite the clear problems in getting service in the system, the main complaint of the participants was that, at the public hospitals, they felt as though they were treated as 'cattle' and 'not as a real person with dignity'. In one interview with a poor black woman who lives in a housing project in the *Zona Norte*, I was told that her former employer had arranged an appointment for her in a private hospital after she had had no success in getting treatment for her hypertension in the public hospital. She commented that at the private hospital she was treated 'like a person', with 'politeness and respect', whereas at the public hospital the doctors and nurses were 'rude' and treated her 'like an animal'.

Conclusion

The women and men who participated in this study did not identify themselves as activists in organised social movements, nor were they involved in political campaigns. They have recast citizenship in terms of the needs and interests of families and communities, in order to contest access to their society's resources. This understanding is more relevant than more conventional understandings of their daily lives.[9] This process of addressing the problems of their own communities, and reinforcing their sense of community at a local level, is the most important form of democratic practice in their view. The women and men whom I interviewed redefined citizenship in their daily lives in three ways:

- as relating more to the 'private' than the public sphere
- as a qualified form of political and economic participation, which privileges their own families and communities
- as dignity in their daily life.

In conclusion, the idea of citizenship for the poor in Rio de Janeiro incorporates aspects of democratic and market logic, but stresses the importance of supporting family and community structures, and participating with dignity in the life of the city. Hannah Arendt makes the point that 'The fundamental deprivation of human rights [and citizenship] is manifested first and above all in the deprivation of a place in the world [a political space] which makes opinions significant, and actions effective...'(Arendt, cited in Jelin 1998, 405). In the absence of opportunities for debate about government and economic policy and its impact on citizenship, participants have developed their own idea of citizenship, with the dignity of individuals, families, and communities at its centre.

Joanna Wheeler is the Research Manager for the Development Research Centre on Citizenship, Participation, and Accountability based at the Institute of Development Studies, University of Sussex, Brighton BN1 9RE, UK.
j.wheeler@ids.ac.uk

Notes

1 Support for this research was provided by the Fulbright Foundation, and I would like to thank Marisa, Rita, and Nilsa from the Rio Fulbright office for their support. Thanks also to Benjamin Junge at Emory University for comments on an earlier version of this paper. Remaining flaws are of my own making.
2 The 1993 plebiscite was mandated by the 1988 constitution as part of the democratic reforms that began in the early 1980s. The plebiscite was an obligatory nationwide vote to endorse a form of government. The options for types of government included presidential democracy, parliamentary democracy, monarchy, and autocracy.
3 Import-substitution subsidies were the basis of much of Latin America's economic policy from the 1960s to the 1980s. The underlying premise of this policy was to impose high tariffs on imports, and simultaneously subsidise national industries in order to promote the domestic production of manufactured goods, for which most countries in Latin America relied on imports.
4 This finding is interesting in light of the fact that various scholars have attributed the lack of women in leadership positions within social movements to patriarchal bias within these movements (Houtzager 2000; Neuhouser 1995). However, this may have more to do with the fact that women in *favelas* understand citizenship and democracy differently from men.
5 Participants were asked: 'Do you participate politically? And if so, what is the most important way you participate?'
6 In terms of democratic impulses, the focus here is on forms of political participation that work for the good of some broader collectivity, rather than promoting representative governance, because that was the notion most commonly elaborated by the study's participants.
7 See www.conhecimentosgerais. com.br/ historia-do-brasil/redemocratizacao. html (last checked by the author 26 November 2003). I would also like to acknowledge Carlos Pio of the Federal University of Brasilia for his correspondence regarding the plebiscite on governance.
8 In February 2003, growing levels of violence, including bombings of government business, mass bus

burnings, and hijackings on major roadways, led to the temporary presence of the military on Rio de Janeiro's streets to enforce public order.

9 Ong (1996, 737) makes a similar argument in reference to Asian immigrants to California.

References

Bulbeck, C. (1998) *Re-orienting Western Feminisms: Women's Diversity in a Post-Colonial World*, Cambridge: Cambridge University Press

Davis, D. (1999) *Avoiding the Dark: Race and the Forging of National Culture in Modern Brazil*, Brookfield, VT: Ashgate

Holston, J. and A. Appadurai (1999) 'Introduction: cities and citizenship', in J. Holston (ed.) *Cities and Citizenship*, Durham, NC: Duke University Press

Houtzager, P. (2000) 'Social movements amidst democratic transitions: lessons from the Brazilian countryside', *The Journal of Development Studies* 36(5): 59-88

Jelin, E. (1998) 'Toward a culture of participation and citizenship: challenges for a more equitable world', in S. Alvarez, E. Dagnino, and A. Escobar (eds.) *Cultures of Politics/Politics of Cultures: Re-visioning Latin American Social Movements*, Boulder, CO: Westview Press

Journal do Brasil (2002) News report, 8 March 2002

Machado, L.T. (1980) *Formação do Brasil e unidade nacional*, São Paulo: Instituto Brasileiro de Difusão Cultural

Marx, A. (1998) *Making Race and Nation: A Comparison of South Africa, the United States, and Brazil*, Cambridge: Cambridge University Press

Neuhouser, K. (1995) '"Worse than men": gendered mobilization in an urban Brazilian squatter settlement, 1971-91', *Gender and Society* 9(1): 38-59

Ong, A. (1996) 'Cultural citizenship as subject-making: immigrants negotiate racial and cultural boundaries in the United States', *Current Anthropology* 37(5): 737

Paoli, M. and V. da Silva Telles (1998) 'Social rights: conflicts in contemporary Brazil', in S. Alvarez, E. Dagnino, and A. Escobar (eds.) *Cultures of Politics/Politics of Cultures: Re-visioning Latin American Social Movements*, Boulder, CO: Westview Press

UNDP (2000) *UNDP Poverty Report 2000*, Washington, DC: United Nations Development Programme

UNDP (2001) *Relatório de Desenvolvimento Humano do Rio de Janeiro 2000*, Rio de Janeiro: United Nations Development Programme

UNECLAC (1997) *Sustainable Development, Poverty and Gender, Latin America and the Caribbean: Working Toward the Year 2000*, Santiago: United Nations Economic Commission for Latin America and the Caribbean

Creating citizens who demand just governance:
gender and development in the twenty-first century

Maitrayee Mukhopadhyay

The issue of good governance assumed enormous significance in debates on global development in the 1990s. By and large, this translated into policies aimed at building accountability of public administration institutions to the broad 'public', but omitted to consider two key issues: first, the 'public' consists of women and men, who have gender-differentiated needs and interests; second, civil-society institutions have a role to play in creating the demand for democratic, accountable, and just governance. To address these omissions, and to reinforce the importance of bringing a gender perspective to global debates and approaches to international development, KIT Gender, at the Royal Tropical Institute in Amsterdam, initiated a three-year programme in 1999. It is entitled 'Gender, Citizenship, and Governance'. This article discusses the programme and its relevance to international development, and provides three case studies from the programme; from India, Bangladesh, and South Africa.

Mainstreaming a gender perspective in development was the overall strategy adopted at the Fourth UN Conference for Women, held in Beijing in 1995, to support the goal of gender equality. The rationale for this strategy is that it is important to bring the goal of gender equality to the centre of the development process. After three decades of gender and development activism, most in development institutions continue to need constant reminders of the need for gender analysis in their work. Why is it that policy makers still have to be lobbied to include the 'g' word, and colleagues need to be convinced that integrating a gender analysis in their work makes a qualitative difference?

There are two ways in which gender equality concerns can be mainstreamed. *Integration* aims to ensure that such concerns are integrated in the analysis of obstacles to development, and that these concerns inform the formulation of policy, programmes, and projects. Specific targets are set for outcomes, and the monitoring and evaluation of policies and programmes must capture the progress made in the achievement of gender equality. For example, an agricultural development project might focus on ensuring that women involved in farming have equal access to technology and information. In contrast, the *transformation* approach aims to move beyond integrating women's concerns relating to the demands of their daily lives, to focus on improving women's position (status), and thereby transforming the agenda. For example, if the key issue facing women in agriculture is lack of independent land rights, this approach would move far beyond ensuring that women have equal access to technology and information, to advocating for changes in inheritance practices and land ownership.

Integration and transformation require work at two different institutional levels. Integration involves working within development institutions to improve the quality of their work – improving the 'supply' side of the equation. A transformative agenda requires efforts to support, nurture, and create constituencies who demand change. To do this, development organisations need to understand the nature of government and of state–society relationships, and the degree of autonomy that policy-making institutions have from international development and financial institutions. In many countries in Africa, for example, social and political movements have marginal influence on what the policy-making institutions are doing, because many governments are dependent not only on the people, but on international support, to stay in power. Working on governance involves understanding the interconnect-edness of institutions at different levels, and determining the role that social movements can play in demanding justice for the poor.

KIT's programme

KIT's programme on gender, citizenship, and governance was set up in order to address such issues. The programme aimed to make gender equity and equality a core concern in governing development. It provided a framework to facilitate innovative gender and governance initiatives in nine countries and in two regions of the world: South Asia (Bangladesh, India, Pakistan, and Sri Lanka) and southern Africa (Namibia, Zambia, South Africa, and Zimbabwe). The programme was under-taken in collaboration with 16 organisations from these countries. The development of these partnerships, and of collaborative action research, was the cornerstone of the programme. The aim was to construct a forum for linking and learning, in the best traditions of participatory and action-oriented research, and contribute the insights generated to improve development policy and practice.

The international development context
In the 1990s, the issue of good governance assumed enormous significance in the debates on global development. One reason for this was the growing realisation on the part of many that conventional development efforts had failed to achieve the desired ends. These were to eliminate poverty and inequality, and promote respect for human rights.

Attention began to shift away from traditional development concerns towards a greater consideration for the way in which power is exercised in the management of economic and social resources for develop-ment. International financial institutions such as the World Bank, bilateral donors, and donor groupings like the European Union (EU) and Organisation for Economic Co-operation and Development/ Develop-ment Assistance Committee (OECD/DAC), highlighted the need for good governance, to ensure that development aid had the desired results of bringing about economic, social, and political changes in developing countries.

Good governance meant different things to the donors and other actors involved in development, according to their different priorities and mandates. However, on the whole, the good-governance agenda aimed to make public administration institutions accountable to the public whom they are supposed to serve. Most money spent by donors in support of good governance in developing countries went towards reforming the state and attempting to improve public administration. Democratic reform concentrated, in the main, on reform of electoral systems, decentralisation and devolution of government, and reform of administrative and legal systems.

Good governance and the international 'crisis of control'
The good-governance agenda did not automatically address the question of gender inequality. For example, establishing the rule of law has not automatically translated into the legal recognition of violence against women as a crime. Similarly, expanding the scope of citizens' participation in governance, by decen-tralising government, has not by itself

ensured that women and men are represented on an equal basis.

The attempts to improve governance took place at a time when the processes of rapid economic globalisation were at their peak. Over the last three decades of the twentieth century, the speed and range of the globalisation of economics, politics, and culture have involved bringing in new-comers into governance. The traditional actors – the state, civil society, and political institutions – have been joined by international development and financial institutions. State capacity to manage the political economy of a country has been seriously undermined in both the North and the South, because of the processes of economic globalisation. Needless to say, Southern countries have suffered more because they start from a position of greater poverty, less social development, inade-quate development of markets and institutions, and weaker bargaining power in international trade and financial systems. The processes of globalisation have resulted in a *crisis of control* in the world order. By this I mean that no single centre of authority has the ability to manage economic and social changes in a way that will take care of those groups of people who are harmed by the changes (for example, those whose livelihoods are lost). The crisis of control, and the negative effects that the current model of global development has had on people's lives, has resulted in movements promoting global justice. These have moved the struggle to rights beyond individual nation states.

One of the more successful instances of global citizen action has been women's activism for rights, equality, and policies that enhance human development and justice for all. Women's constituencies have emerged as global citizens, arguing for the right to development, freedom from domestic and sexual violence, sexual and reproductive rights, and the implementation of the Convention on the Elimination of all Forms of Discrimination against Women (CEDAW) and the Beijing Platform for Action.

While global citizen action has been necessary to provide the wider political environment for the construction of new rights, entrenching these rights has involved hard work at local and national levels. It has been necessary to work with powerful institutions to change the rules and to demand responsiveness and accountability. This has meant working within the political spaces provided by these institutions, and also constructing new political spaces.

Gender, citizenship, and governance: what did we do?

In the KIT programme we have focused on three areas of concern: taking office, engendering governance institutions, and claiming citizenship. Organisations which have participated in KIT's Gender, Citizen-ship, and Governance programme have adopted a three-pronged strategy, consisting of the following elements:

- creating access to governance institutions

- effecting change within these institutions to improve their ability to respond to women's needs and interests

- staking women's claim to new entitlements, arising from the needs articulated by those women affected by lack of rights and influence.

The organisations have worked hard to bring about changes in institutional practices that would help women to secure their strategic gender interests. The projects undertaken by these organisations have not been limited to advocating decentralisation of government, or getting more women into government and political office, or reforming the law. Rather, the participating organisations have intervened in these areas with the objective of reforming and rewriting the 'rules of the game'. The case studies presented here illuminate what is involved.

India: building political legitimacy for minority women in local government

In India, the question of representation of disadvantaged groups has been debated in political circles since independence in 1947, with caste-based discrimination as the major concern. The Indian Constitution banned discrimination on the basis of caste and included those castes that had historically been wronged and treated as 'untouchables' in a special schedule of the Constitution. These caste groups came to be known as 'scheduled castes', and quotas were instituted for their representation in Parliament, state assemblies, the public sector, and in educational institutions. In 1993 the 73rd and 74th amendments to the Constitution were passed, making Local Self Governing Institutions (LSGIs) mandatory as part of government. A uniform three-tier system – district; *taluk*/block (a cluster of villages); and village levels in the rural areas or Municipalities and Corporations in large urban centres – came into formal existence. An important aspect of the amendment was that one-third of the seats in all levels of local government was reserved for the election of women. In the following year, 350,000 women entered local government as elected representatives. Civil-society groups rallied to support the new incumbents, offering training in order to enhance their effectiveness.

The Confederation of Voluntary Associations (COVA) – a non-government organisation based in Hyderabad, south India – is one of the NGOs that took up work in this area. COVA saw that the opportunity presented to women to become political agents and address women's gender-specific concerns was not being realised, despite the large numbers of women entering local government as a result of the quotas. COVA was particularly concerned about the effectiveness of women representatives from Muslim, *Dalit*, and other marginalised groupings.

COVA saw its main task as establishing the legitimacy of female political representatives, in a context where the dice were loaded against women on two counts. First, political parties and male representatives saw the women representatives as entering political office on the basis of favours by government, rather than on account of their leadership qualities. Second, political parties and individual politicians had captured the reserved seats for women by placing 'proxy women' in these seats. These were women who did not take active office, but whose men (usually husbands) did this for them.

COVA's strategy was to hold four workshops for a core group of women representatives. The workshops were held at six-month intervals, and aimed to support the women and foster a sense of accountability to their constituents. The training focused on ensuring that women gained a better understanding of rules and procedures, and developed skills such as public speaking, interaction with the media, and interaction with government officials. COVA produced an information handbook for each participant.

In between the workshops, the women representatives were required by COVA to put their training into practice by meeting their constituents and engaging with local administration officials, political parties, and the media. The women's performance was monitored by COVA, whose representatives met with constituents, officials, political parties, and the media to get a sense of whether perceptions of the political representatives were shifting. This monitoring acted as a further impetus for the women representatives to undertake the agreed tasks.

For the first time, the women political representatives visited constituents unaccompanied by male relatives. They also began to engage with officials, and address council meetings and the media. This gained them respect as leaders, which in turn improved their confidence and self-esteem. At the second workshop, the majority said they were not interested in continuing a career in politics; by the fourth workshop, the majority were interested. The women representatives now saw themselves as legitimate political actors, and this reinforced the perceptions of others that women were to be taken seriously as political leaders.

The case of Ameena, who participated in this programme, illustrates both the possibilities and difficulties of establishing women as legitimate political actors. Women's position in relation to men shapes the nature of their political participation. Ameena came to be a political representative at the instigation of her husband and the local Member of the Legislative Assembly (MLA).[1] Her husband had always been active in politics; he was a former councillor for his wife's ward, and the City President of the Minority Cell of the Congress Party. He was planning to contest the election, but when the ward was reserved for women, he asked his wife to stand. She was not interested in politics and declined, but the elders of the area, including the local MLA, pressed her. Ameena reluctantly agreed, although she was a little scared and tense about taking on the job.

Ameena's husband undertook a door-to-door campaign, with six women of the area, covering 1,000 houses. She won by 987 votes, the highest margin of victory in the history of the ward. Her husband motivates her to visit the field and meet with officials on her own, and also encouraged her to participate in the trainings organised by COVA. He feels that his wife is capable of discharging her responsibilities without support, and he does not interfere with her activities and freedom of movement. However, he says that he does not feel like sharing domestic work, because he has never done this and it is not a man's role. Unlike men, women entering politics have to manage both roles – their new role as public representative and their traditional role of caring and being

responsible for the family. This imposes special limitations on women's participation in politics and in public life, limitations that men do not face. Thus, while Ameena's husband was extremely helpful in furthering her public role, her private/domestic role was seen by him, and by the larger society, as something that women, in order to be 'women', are obliged to do. Ameena's participation in the COVA programme helped to open up discussion about gender roles, and this is a first step towards change. Her husband had never before been confronted with the 'taken for granted' nature of gender roles and relations.

Ameena is a graduate in Home Science, was active during school and college days, and successful in many quizzes and debating competitions. Despite her education and experience in public speaking, she felt a little scared during the Municipal Corporation meetings and did not speak in the first three meetings. By the fourth meeting, she decided to move a resolution about a civic problem in her area. She was the first woman to speak in the Corporation meetings. Gradually others also started speaking, and now women take an active part in the proceedings.

Ameena now says she wants to continue in politics, and does not want to become a housewife again. She admits that earlier she never used to read about politics in the newspapers, but now the first thing she reads is the political news. However, her constituency will not remain reserved for women during the next elections, and her husband is keen to contest this seat himself. Under the circumstances, Ameena may not contest the elections and may have to make way for her husband, in order to keep peace in family relations.

Bangladesh: ensuring accountability of health-service providers to stakeholders

Naripokkho is a women's rights organisation based in Bangladesh. Founded in 1983, it has established a reputation as an advocacy group for women's health and rights. Bangladesh has a very high maternal mortality ratio, at 450 per 100,000 live births. These deaths are largely due to preventable causes. The statistic shows the failure of the public health system to provide effective services for women.

Around 1979, primary health care in Bangladesh was organised around the *upazila* (sub-district level). The Upazila Health Complex (UHC) is the comprehensive primary health-service provider institution, and is administered by the Upazila Health and Family Planning Officer, who convenes the Upazila Health Advisory Committee (UHAC) which is to be chaired by the local Member of Parliament. The Committee, which should have representation from the providers (government health officials), citizens, and elected representatives in local government institutions, is supposed to meet every month. Its objective is to improve health and medical services at the hospital that it serves and solve any problems that might arise at the local level. Naripokkho worked in one *upazila*, Pathorghata, in collaboration with a local NGO, to improve the response of the government health-service providers to women's reproductive health needs. The UHAC of Pathorghata was defunct, with no meetings having been convened for five years. Doctors took fees from patients at the UHC for services they were supposed to provide free, and sometimes resorted to extortion.

Naripokkho explored how the forum offered by the monthly meeting of UHAC could be used to enforce accountability on a sustainable basis. The organisation made a series of strategic choices about the most effective ways to stimulate debate about women having a right to health care, and acceptance of this as a principle, through the forum of the UHAC. This included ensuring that all members had faith in using the UHAC as a problem-solving forum, as well as ensuring respect for its decisions, especially on the part of health-care

providers. At the outset, Naripokkho chose to engage first with the concerned local official, rather than engaging with the Ministry, which would have resulted in top-down directives.

Following this, Naripokkho encouraged stakeholders to see the UHAC as a body that could address and solve some of the problems being raised, and to see its meetings as an 'invited space' for citizens to participate in decision making. Naripokkho built up support among the stakeholders for the revived UHAC, so that it could actually start functioning, and service providers and users could support each other in problem solving. Since this was an effort to strengthen 'citizen voice' as well as 'state response', it was important to involve diverse actors. These included women from the community, NGOs, elected representatives, the doctors of the UHC, journalists, other health practitioners, and the local government administration.

Naripokkho also engaged with the local elected representatives, since they were already motivated to improve women's health and rights, and were also members of the UHAC. As such, they were accountable to their electorate. They monitored compliance with the decisions of the UHAC. This was very effective, as it was based on the power of the 'public mandate' of elected representatives to take decisions on behalf of their constituencies. Journalists helped by creating a public debate about the need for health providers to be accountable to users, no matter how poor. This was very effective: whenever there was a lapse in service, there was immediate media coverage. This enforced compliance with the agreements of the UHAC, since anyone violating the norms risked exposure and public embarrassment.

Some significant results of the project include enhanced and proactive participation of the UHAC members in the committee meetings; monitoring of hospital practices by the journalists and councillors; improved professional behaviour on the part of the doctors; better service provision (for example, fewer instances of bribery, and regular health education classes); and encouragement for women to negotiate lower fees for consulting the doctors.

South Africa: reform of customary law

The Centre for Applied Legal Studies (CALS) is a research organisation at the University of Witwatersrand, South Africa. The Gender and Research Project (GRP) at CALS was formed in 1992. It had the broad objectives of promoting gender equality and human rights. From its inception, the GRP was involved in the negotiations about the new South African Constitution. It provided technical assistance to the Women's National Coalition, and to women in the African National Congress (ANC), which formed the first democratically elected government. It also played a role in one of the key disputes during these negotiations, which was the place of customary law in the Constitution.

Customary law is a set of rules and practices which governs the lives of the majority of black South Africans. Prior to the onset of democracy in 1994, customary law did not enjoy a status equal to civil law. The customary system, which was not codified before colonial rule, had been manipulated by successive white governments, in collaboration with state-supported male elders, into a codified system which entrenched and extended the subordination of women.

In 1995, the Rural Women's Movement (RWM) identified reform of customary marriage as a key priority, and asked CALS to conduct research and advocacy with them on this topic. CALS began a research project which sought to identify the practices, needs, and interests of women in relation to customary marriage. It documented the experience of women who had married under customary law, as well as their attitudes towards their marital status, and to the idea of reform. CALS believed that the information collected would provide a basis for influencing the state to reform customary laws on marriage. It hoped that the result would be a law that would meet the needs of women. When the South African Law Commission (SALC) started investigating reforms to customary law in 1996, CALS engaged in this process through providing a written submission, oral advocacy, and attending SALC meetings and workshops. It relied on the research undertaken to inform the process. CALS also hoped that women who were involved in the research (especially those who were part of an organised constituency) would go on to participate in the democratic process.

One issue – that of polygyny, in which one man marries two or more women – caused much debate within CALS and the RWM. The RWM and CALS research findings overwhelmingly showed the practice to be oppressive to women. However, questions were raised about whether or not prohibition of polygyny should be called for. Certain events caused CALS to rethink the issue. Significant here was the annual general meeting of the RWM in February 1998, where members were chanting the slogan 'one man, one woman'. CALS noticed that some members sat quietly, without chanting the slogan. When asked why they did not chant, they replied that they were living in polygynous relationships, and this prevented them from chanting the slogan. During discussions facilitated by CALS, the divisiveness of the slogan was raised. CALS became aware that women were not a homogeneous group, and they were not condemning polygyny with one voice. It was critical to ensure that the law offered protection to women and children in existing polygynous households. In the CALS research, enormous concern had been expressed about the rights of women and children to property in polygynous marriages. Prohibition of polygyny might result in making wives and children even more vulnerable and marginalised.

When the Bill was finally tabled in Parliament, CALS had to make a series of strategic choices about its content. The Bill provided for equality within customary marriage, reflecting the wishes of women for marriages that gave them legal security (especially in respect of property), while enabling them to maintain positive cultural links. The Bill sought to contribute to the decline of the practice of polygyny, yet protect vulnerable women in polygynous unions. The Bill did not reflect all CALS' proposals, and aspects of it were controversial (especially the provisions on polygyny).

However, CALS was aware of the compromises and choices that had been made during the SALC process, as well as the lengthy process of research and consultation. CALS decided to support the Bill, and focused on its strengths, while highlighting the concerns of rural women. The Bill was fast-tracked through Parliament, which meant that the resultant Recognition of Customary Marriages Act was made operational only two years after its enactment in November 2000.

The engagement of CALS did not end here: the organisation was particularly concerned to examine the way in which the Act was implemented, from the perspective of women using it. Given that the law had been structured around the expressed needs of women, did it actually address these needs, and solve the previously identified problems of minority legal status, which affected access to property during marriage, lack of decision making power, and non-consensual polygyny? To measure this, CALS began to collect information on how the Act affects the lives of women connected to the original research sites. CALS also interviewed officials responsible for implementing the Act. A number of problems with implementation came to light through the monitoring research; for each of the problems identified, CALS has sought to engage the stakeholders to seek solutions.

Governing for equity: lessons learned

We at KIT began the Gender, Citizenship, and Governance programme with the intention of contributing to the generation of knowledge and practice that would help to make gender equity and equality a core concern in governing development. Through their action-research projects, participating organisations arrived at understandings and definitions of good governance from a gender perspective.

The meaning of good governance from a gender perspective

We found that 'women taking political office' means not only creating mechanisms for their entry into public office. It also means establishing women as legitimate political actors, as opposed to private persons who do not have a place in politics and the public sphere.

'Engendering' the institutions of national governance means ensuring that they are accountable to women as citizens; changing rules, procedures, and priorities that exclude the participation of poor women and the incorporation of their interests in the development agenda; and mobilising and organising women's voices in civil society.

The meaning of citizenship

What does citizenship mean for poor women? First, we found that it means the right to participate and to be agents. For groups on the margins of society, citizenship means acquiring the power and understanding to define the problem of lack of rights, and the solutions to this problem.

Second, it means aspiring to substantive equality, as opposed to formal equality. The case studies highlight the need to be pragmatic, and discuss and analyse rights according to the priorities of the affected population, rather than relying on orthodoxies about women's rights. However, this is not to suggest that we should promote cultural relativism. Rather, as the case studies show, this is a way of finding a successful way to struggle for substantive equality – and make rights real. It involves honestly understanding and representing the lived experience of specific categories of women (the most marginalised, or those who are most affected by lack of specific rights). It means moving away from the idea that women's interests are only about gender relations – that is, about women in relation to men – towards a more nuanced understanding of the specificities of a woman's position, the construction of which depends on other social relations (for example, race). The best illustration of this is the case study of customary-law reform undertaken by CALS in South Africa. In its work on reforming customary law, CALS established that women's experiences and needs must be the key to the reform process. The organisation moved away from a universalistic idea of women and women's interests, once it was made aware of the realities of women who lived in polygynous marriages.

The practice of good governance

Constructing voice

Women face barriers which restrict their claims to citizenship, preventing them from participation in politics and the institutions of governance. To break through these, they need to have a voice, and organise as a political constituency within civil society. The projects outlined here all helped to articulate the voices of the most marginalised women, by highlighting real-life experiences of exclusion from entitlements and rights.

Creating 'communities of struggle'

The case studies highlight the important role of a political constituency of women in building awareness. This awareness is key to creating a public which is broadly sympathetic to the principle of gender equality, and in challenging prevailing notions of women's subordination. In order to give voice to women's demands, an immense amount of work has to take place, to organise and mobilise constituencies that grow into an awareness of the right to have a right, and the right to participate in decisions affecting one's life.

Shaping the accountability interface

'Constructing and articulating voice' does not necessarily lead to better outcomes for women. The case studies highlight the significance of ensuring that this voice is heard by the institutions that affect the lives of citizens, so that changes take place, and there is an accountability and responsiveness from these institutions. The project undertaken by Naripokkho sought to develop the accountability of local health-service providers to women. Naripokkho did this through a gamut of strategies, which included giving providers a voice to articulate their problems; reviving a defunct health-accountability body and making it function as a problem-solving body, including multiple stakeholders; and providing information about women's health needs so that the service providers were aware of what they had to address.

Carving out space

The projects discussed here also demonstrate the importance of carving out spaces which enable women to articulate their interests, and provide an 'accountability interface' between interests and institutions of governance. Sometimes these spaces are opened up by decision-making institutions, and at other times spaces have to be created through women's own efforts. The projects constructed, created, and, on occasion, opened up spaces that were by all accounts closed to public participation.

Working on both sides: in and out of the state

On the one hand, women in civil society need to become more aware of their rights and more aware of how to hold institutions to account. On the other, women need to work within institutions of governance to reshape how they function. Most of the projects worked in tandem with state institutions, sometimes aligning with the agenda of the state, and other times agitating for change.

Establishing authority through contributing knowledge

In all cases, the organisations which participated in our programme were able to engage with civil society and state actors as they did because of the legitimacy and authority that they had established through their active contributions. Some organisations, like the International Centre for Ethnic Studies (ICES) in Sri Lanka, and Sister in Namibia, worked to increase the number of women elected to political office, and undertook research into the kinds of electoral system and mechanism that would be needed to increase women's access to political office. CALS in South Africa became an important resource for the SALC, because of the extensive research that it had undertaken to identify the practices, needs, and interests of black women in relation to marriage. PRIP Trust in Bangladesh and Sakhi in India researched the structures and functioning of local government institutions, and was able to suggest with authority changes that would enable both women and men elected to these institutions to perform their roles. Naripokkho in Bangladesh researched and provided information on women's needs to the local health-accountability forum set up to monitor health-care provision.

Understanding institutions and whose interests they represent

The projects demonstrate that once civil-society organisations have insinuated their way into the functioning of governance institutions, a main task is to make transparent the manner in which the institution functions, how decisions are made, and how resources are allocated. Bringing poor women's needs and interests to bear on the agenda of decision-making institutions makes visible the deficiencies of the structures and processes that make up

these institutions. PRIP Trust in Bangladesh did this by involving elected representatives of local government bodies in a resource-mapping exercise; undertaking a situational analysis of how these function, and presenting the results to the stakeholders; and organising workshops and meetings to develop the capacity of elected members. In the process, undemocratic practices were unearthed, the marginalisation of elected women representatives was made visible, and information regarding resources available to local government was more widely shared.

All the action-research projects highlight the importance of understanding organisations of state bureaucracy, their structures, and processes of policy formulation, planning, and implementation, in order to locate strategic entry points – in terms of location and timing – for beginning to turn around seemingly monolithic organisations, to make them operate in ways that are aware of, and accountable to, the interests of poor women.

Decentralisation of government is being offered as the panacea to improve governance, make governance transparent and participatory, and bring government structures closer to people and therefore make them more relevant to people's lives. The experiences of the action-research projects that have worked with local government institutions have helped to destroy many of these myths, precisely because the myths have been interrogated from the point of view of women. This process has shown the following.

First, since local government is more embedded in local social structures than national government, and since prevailing gender ideologies are more concentrated at the local level, it is more difficult for women to penetrate as independent political actors, or for them to raise controversial gender issues at this level.

Second, the experiences with local government institutions highlighted that, even where attempts are made to put in place structures for people's participation in these institutions, this does not mean that women are taken into account. Procedures were found to be gender-neutral and gender-blind in decentralised development, despite strict guidelines for democratic decision making, women's participation, and budgetary allocations. There was the incorrect assumption that women and men have equal power and status, and the model of development did not consider the need to transform unequal gender relations.

Maitrayee Mukhopadhyay is the Area Leader for Social Development and Gender Equity in the Department of Development Policy and Practice at the Royal Tropical Institute, Amsterdam. In the last four years she has developed a special focus on citizenship and participatory governance, and its relevance to development policy and practice. Address: Royal Tropical Institute, PO Box 95001, 1090 HA Amsterdam, The Netherlands.
m.mukhopadhyay@kit.nl

Notes

1 India consists of 25 states, each with its own legislature with elected representatives. An elected representative to a state legislature is called Member of the Legislative Assembly.

Bibliography

This article draws on all the following sources:

Budlender, D. (ed.) (1997) *The Second Women's Budget,* Cape Town: Idasa

Edwards, M. and J. Gaventa (eds.) (2001) *Global Citizen Action*, London: Earthscan

Goetz, A.M. and D. O'Brien (1995) 'Governing for the common wealth? The World Bank's approach to poverty and governance', *IDS Bulletin* 26(2): 17-27

Jahan, R. (1995) *The Elusive Agenda: Mainstreaming Women in Development*, London: Zed Books

Kabeer, N. (2002) 'Citizenship, affiliation and exclusion: perspectives from the south', *IDS Bulletin* 23(2): 12-23

Lister, R. (1997a) *Citizenship: Feminist Perspectives*, Basingstoke: Macmillan

Lister, R. (1997b) 'Citizenship: towards a feminist synthesis', *Feminist Review* 57: 28-47

Lister, R. (1998) 'Citizen in action: citizenship and community development in Northern Ireland context', *Community Development Journal* 33(3): 226-35

Mukhopadhyay, M. (1998a) *Legally Dispossessed: Gender, Identity and the Process of Law,* Calcutta: Stree

Mukhopadhyay, M. (1998b) 'Gender equity and equality: the agenda for good governance', *Connections* 10: 16-20

Mukhopadhyay, M. (2003) *Governing for Equity*, Amsterdam: KIT Press/Oxfam Publications

Mbatha, L. (2002) 'Reforming the customary law of succession', *South African Journal on Human Rights* 18(2): 259-86

Nunnenkamp, P. (1995) 'What donors mean by good governance: heroic ends, limited means, and traditional dilemmas of development cooperation', *IDS Bulletin* 26(2): 9-16

O'Brien, R. et al. (eds.) (2000) *Contesting Global Governance: Multilateral Economic*

56

Institutions and Global Social Movements, Cambridge: Cambridge University Press

Pateman, C. (1992) 'The patriarchal welfare state' in L. McDowell and R. Pringle (eds.) *Defining Women: Social Institutions and Gender Divisions*, Cambridge: Polity Press

Phillips, A. (1992) 'Feminism, equality and difference' in L. McDowell and R. Pringle (eds.) *Defining Women: Social Institutions and Gender Divisions*, Cambridge: Polity Press

Phillips, A. (1993) *Democracy and Difference*, Cambridge: Polity Press

Robinson, M. (1995) 'Introduction: towards democratic governance', *IDS Bulletin* 26(2): 1-9

Sen, A. (1997) 'Human capital and human capability', *World Development* 25(12): 1959-61

Sen, A. and J. Drèze (1995) *India: Economic Development and Social Opportunity*, New Delhi: Oxford University Press

Sen, G. (1997a) 'Globalization in the 21st Century: Challenges for Civil Society', The UvA Development Lecture, Amsterdam, 1997

Sen, G. (1997b) 'Globalization, justice and equity: a gender perspective', *Development* 40(2): 21-26

United Nations (1995) *Beijing Platform for Action*, Fourth World Conference on Women

White, G. (1995) 'Towards a democratic developmental state', *IDS Bulletin* 26(2): 27-35

Fragmented feminisms:
women's organisations and citizenship in 'transition' in Poland

Angela Coyle

Both governments and international donors now increasingly recognise women's organisations as key actors in the promotion of women's rights, democracy, and citizenship. Yet they remain, on the whole, poorly equipped for this role. The precarious, under-funded, and short-term existence of most women's organisations does not equate with a flourishing civil society. If women's organisations are to have more impact, they and their sponsors need to develop a longer view. This article focuses on the author's experience of capacity-building work with four women's organisations in Poland. Here, women's citizenship and rights are being promoted in the context of neo-liberal economic policies.

For more than a decade I have run management training and capacity-building courses for women's organisations in many different parts of the world, including the Caribbean, South Asia, Africa, and Central and Eastern Europe. This work has given me access to a very diverse range of women's organisations, and an unusually privileged vantage point from which to consider the nature of their work and activities, their experiences and struggles, and, indeed, the highs and lows of trying to change the world on behalf of women. The more I do this work, the more I am troubled by the precarious and insecure conditions under which women's organisations function.

In this article I draw on my experience of a capacity-building project that I carried out with four women's organisations in Poland. This showed me once again how tiny, under-funded, often volunteer-based women's organisations are frequently expected by donors to challenge governments which are indifferent, or even hostile, to women's rights. No matter how well run they are, how

they can do this effectively is not at all obvious.

Women's organisations and 'global' citizenship

Since the 1980s, international development agencies have shifted their funding strategy away from direct aid to governments, in favour of funding non-government organisations (NGOs). NGOs have come to be regarded as a cheaper, less bureaucratic, and more controllable form of intervention. They are often also favoured as a focus for local, 'grassroots' social activism and public participation. They are seen as providing the 'bottom-up development' that donor agencies now consider necessary for the construction of civil society and democratisation (Edwards and Hulme 1996). Women's organisations have also benefited from this new and extended international sponsorship (Pearson and Jackson 1998). Over the last two decades, women's organisations have sprung up all over the world.

They are now active on a whole range of issues, giving voice to many concerns that did not previously appear on any development agenda. They also provide services for women and their families that governments cannot – or will not – provide.

The UN world conferences on women's rights and empowerment have been especially important in promoting women's organisations as a renewed focus for women's activism (Wichterich 1998). They have fostered a new international dialogue between women's organisations, and have encouraged states to adopt national gender-equality plans and national forums through which women's organisations can engage with their own national governments. The UK government's Department for International Development (DFID) refers to women's organisations as 'key actors' in its strategy for promoting the empowerment of women (DFID 2000, 23). This is especially the case in those countries and regions where women's economic and political participation is restricted, and NGOs often provide the only available platform for women's public participation.

However, while women's organisations may now be widely favoured as a vehicle for promoting active citizenship, democratisation, and social change, they are often not well equipped for sustained activity on behalf of women (Coyle 2001). First, it is well recognised that many women's organisations suffer from being small, ineffectively managed, and inadequately and precariously funded (Cockburn 2001; Grant 2001). Nicky Charles has observed that women's organisations are good at innovation, but not so successful at ensuring their own long-term survival (Charles 2000).

Second, we are now in an epoch distinguished by the growth of a 'global' market economy, and the imposition of market-driven structural adjustment policies (SAPs), which have dramatically altered the context in which women's organisations work. The spread of neo-liberal economic management in both developing countries of the South and the 'transition' countries of Central and Eastern Europe has led to increased social fragmentation (Castells 1998; Gray 1998).

Of markets, women, and the 'turn to democracy'

Over the last decade, there has been a concerted international effort to support the 'transition' countries of Central and Eastern Europe to combine economic reform with processes of democratisation and the rebuilding of civil society. The restructuring of the communist system has not had the same effect across all Central and Eastern European countries, but all of them have seen the transformation of the economy from a system of state economic management to a neo-liberal free-market economy, opened up to Western investment. At a political level, single-party systems have been replaced by multi-party systems, and free association and a strong civil society have been promoted.

In principle, there should be a real opportunity for women's organisations in these countries to engage actively with governments, promoting women's rights and citizenship. However, the end of the communist system and the 'turn to democracy' across the entire Central and Eastern Europe region has led to a transformation and reversal in women's fortunes (International Helsinki Federation 2000). The countries of Central and Eastern Europe, and Poland in particular, provide us with a timely reminder that the promotion of women's rights and citizenship is not necessarily a story of linear progress and consolidation. Women have been adversely affected directly by the 'shock therapy' of economic change, and also by 'the revision of all things communist', including the formal commitment of those regimes to equality for women (Molyneux 1996, 234). Women's lives under the former Soviet Union system were unquestionably marked by gender discrimination and especially by the dual burden of work and family responsibilities. Yet, formally at least, women had many of the rights for which Western feminists have long campaigned, including full employment, free child-care provision, and freely available contraception and abortion (Einhorn 1991; Fuszara 1997).

Poland: an anti-feminist state

With support from the International Monetary Fund (IMF), the World Bank, and the European Union (EU), Poland embarked on a radical programme of rapid marketisation and economic transformation in the early 1990s. Now, it is regarded as the model for this kind of fiscal reform, and the most successful of the 'transition' countries in Central and Eastern Europe preparing to join the EU in 2004. Yet, in conjunction with conservative pro-family social policy, economic transformation has given rise to an economic, political, and social context in which it is particularly difficult for women's organisations to act. Organisations that promote women's rights now find themselves contesting the Polish state.

Citizenship and women's rights are principles of a modern democratic state. Yet, in Poland, the marketisation of the economy has been accompanied by an authoritarian rather than democratic state (as predicted by Gray 1998), and by a political culture which promotes the interests of men (Watson 1996). Not only does discrimination against women in the labour market continue to flourish, but inequality and the reinstatement of men as family breadwinners is the official policy solution for high levels of male unemployment, escalating family poverty, and domestic violence.

Although Poland signed up to the UN Beijing Platform for Action, successive governments have done little to promote gender equality, and the national institutional framework established for promoting

women's rights has been systematically dismantled. The post-Beijing National Plan of Action for Women is now suspended, and inquiries from both NGOs and the United Nations on the implementation of the Platform for Action have been ignored (Women's Rights Centre 2000). Hopes that accession negotiations with the EU might encourage the Polish government to carry out a more active policy on gender equality have not materialised either. On the contrary, Poland has done nothing to adjust its legislation to EU standards on the equal treatment of women and men (ibid.).

The Office of the Plenipotentiary[1] for Women, set up in Poland in 1986, went through a number of reincarnations until November 1997, when it was reinvented as the new Plenipotentiary for the Family. It was given a new mandate, which no longer includes working for the advancement of women or gender equality. At the same time, the Forum for Co-operation with Women's Organisations (established in 1996, after the Beijing conference) was disbanded. A national project for combating domestic violence has been replaced with a new programme for providing family support to deal with 'interpersonal aggression'. Domestic violence is presented as 'a gender-neutral phenomenon' (ibid., 5). On cancelling the original project, the Office of the Plenipotentiary stated that 'offering to help women and children outside their family home contributes to the break up of that family' (International Helsinki Federation 2000, 334).

In 1998, the United Nations Committee on Economic, Social, and Cultural Rights, and the United Nations Human Rights Committee, expressed concern in particular at the influence of Roman Catholicism on social policy, and on Poland's very restrictive anti-abortion legislation. These committees also expressed concern about the lack of government action on the growing problems of domestic violence and the trafficking of women, and about continuing inequalities in the labour market, including lower wages for women and discriminatory practices such as pre-employment pregnancy tests (ibid.). The Human Rights Commissioner of The Council of Europe has twice censured Poland for its unconstitutional restriction of abortion rights, but the Polish government has rejected all such criticism as 'foreign interference' (Molyneux 1996, 253).

Feminism in the global age

International support has helped the growth of women's organisations and networks, especially at an international level. In the global age, women's organisations are more prolific and better networked than ever before, but this has not helped most women's organisations to deal better with their local and national political contexts. Paradoxically, the conditions that have led to the rapid expansion of women's organisations are also those that have undermined their capacity to be effective. International sponsorship, and especially the Beijing world conference, has seen the spread of women's organisations 'to the farthest corner of this patriarchal planet' (Wichterich 1998, 147), yet they lack the 'ideas, strategies or instruments for acting on governments in the context of market economies' (ibid., 156).

In both development and gender-equality work, progress is commonly assumed to be rational and linear, and a thriving NGO sector is regarded as evidence of a healthy civil society and democratisation (Escobar 1995; Forbes 2002). In fact, however, women's organisations are operating in a new political context, marked by conflict and fragmentation. Cynthia Cockburn's research in post-war Bosnia-Herzegovina has shown that although women's organisations are potentially valuable in assisting democratisation, in a context in which local government is weak and national government is ill-disposed to the NGO sector, they are scarcely able to play this role (Cockburn 2001).

Donors are, of course, aware of NGOs' weak capacity, and have put in place a range of support mechanisms intended to encourage better planning and project management, and increased accountability and transparency. Often, however, such support is experienced only as bureaucratic, inflexible control (Biggs and Neame 1996), which is increasingly unhelpful in the rapidly changing, insecure, and risk-laden environment which now confronts women's organisations.

Strengthening women's organisations in Poland

It is estimated that there are more than 200 women's groups and organisations active in Poland. All have come into existence since the communist regime ended in 1989. Many of these 'new' groups are actually a reconfiguration of conservative, Catholic, and pro-family groups, that were suppressed during the communist era (Fuszara 1997). There is, however, a handful of Polish women's organisations, supported mostly by external international funding, which would regard themselves as part of the new international women's network (Stienstra 2000). They have been active on a whole range of issues, including violence against women, the trafficking of women, equal rights at work, women's political representation, sexual health, and reproductive rights. The activities of these groups are dependent on the work of volunteers or short-project funding. There is little co-operation between them, and they compete with one another over the limited international funding available.

Throughout 2000, I carried out a capacity-building project, funded by the British Council in Poland, with four women's organisations in Poland. All four organisations have an agenda of promoting women's rights of some kind. As such, they are in opposition to the political *status quo* in Poland. Three of the organisations have been active over a number of years, and are made up of professional women who are well networked with other women's organisations, both nationally and internationally. They have variously campaigned on issues concerning women's employment, political rights and representation, and abortion rights. In order to protect their identities, I shall call the three organisations Women and Work, Women and Politics, and Women's Rights.

In 2000, at the time of the capacity-building project, two organisations – Women's Rights, and Women and Work – had some short-term project funding, and each had a small team of paid workers (three and four respectively). Both groups had moved away from campaigning, and had become more focused on undertaking training, education, research, and the provision of information. Women and Politics continued to define itself as a campaigning group, but, as an informal network without any funding, its actions could only aim to be visible, small-scale, and sporadic. The fourth organisation – which I shall call Refuge – was a newly established self-help group of working-class women who had come together to provide a telephone helpline for women suffering domestic violence. It too had no funding.

The content and method of the project was not decided in advance by the sponsors or the consultants, but in collaboration with the participating groups, who were able to negotiate what they wanted from the project. The project took the form of six weekends of consultancy meetings, held over a 12-month period. During the meetings, each organisation worked with a consultant to identify and analyse its internal organisational ways of working. Alongside these meetings, all four organisations met on a regular basis to consider both common strategic concerns, and methods of collaborative working.

Each organisation identified a range of issues which currently confronted it. These were rooted in the organisations' individual organisational histories and ways of working. The three longer-established organisations all identified problems associated with the difficulties of long-term sustainability, at a time when international funding is moving away from Poland to other regions of the world. They came to recognise those aspects of their current ways of working that militate against coherent leadership, strategic direction, and decision making. They analysed the current dysfunction in their management processes, and identified possible solutions. Meetings, the issue of leadership, working with volunteers, project planning and management, and stakeholder management were among the many issues that the groups wanted to address.

During the consultancy period, Women and Politics appointed a new leader, and produced written job descriptions with roles and responsibilities for core network members. It set up a regular meeting structure as a forum for planning, decision making, and discussion, and looked for an office and meeting place. Women and Work also set up a new regular meeting structure, and with such a forum in place it found that it was surprisingly easy to discuss issues and negotiate differences openly. It found that the new meeting structure improved communications, decision making, and planning, and helped to shift the emphasis from individual to team working.

In contrast, Refuge was concerned with the problems of start-up and early development. It emerged as an NGO that is functioning well as a 'young', volunteer-led organisation, with a management board that meets weekly. Refuge used the project to help to develop its organisational profile, and build up networks with potential funders and sponsors. During the project, Refuge secured a grant from its local municipal council, to produce a range of publicity materials and to hold a national conference.

The consultancy sessions went well beyond the usual parameters of a capacity-building programme. Although all four organisations had participated in capacity-building and management training courses before, the sessions were something of a revelation to these groups.

'It was a kind of journey of discovery. That you can look at an organisation in terms of how it works and functions. We realised from this perspective that there were obstacles interfering with how we worked. We came to understand a lot about ourselves. We had the opportunity to evaluate our own stage of development as an organisation and to think about where we wanted to be.'
(Women and Work, project evaluation)

'The project has helped us bring about good changes within our organisation, in spite of its very informal nature. We now have a new leader, regular meetings and we are looking for a new office/meeting place. We have learned the value of analysing and assessing the ways in which we work and we now have better planning of our activities.'
(Women and Politics, project evaluation)

It was pleasing to see changes occur, but there remained many issues that could not be addressed by the project in the limited time available. It seemed that we had left teams more able to analyse their own management processes and identify problems and their solutions, but it was not certain whether they would use these abilities once the consultancy meetings ended. Women's Rights had come to see the problems arising from its methods of working, but found it difficult to move beyond the diagnostic stage. Its project workers had liked being an informal and innovative group, and stated that they had little interest in running an organisation (which they knew would require more effective management skills, project development, planning, and systems development), or in running campaigns in a hostile political and social climate. During the course of the project, Women and Work abandoned its new meeting structure, and its workers went back to individual and reactive ways of working. The consultancy sessions gave Refuge recognition and endorsement of its effective ways of working, but at some stage in the future the organisation will need to manage its growth and turn into an organisation that employs staff. This will necessarily change current roles and responsibilities, ways of working, and dynamics between its workers.

Developing partnerships and strategic alliances

The development of women's organisations has been encouraged but not planned in Poland; and, in the *ad hoc*, overpopulated terrain of the NGO sector, they are forced into competition with one another for limited funding. This militates against partnership working and strategic alliances. Donors do try to encourage NGOs to work together, by making funding conditional on collaboration. On the whole, such 'forced marriages' have not helped NGOs to appreciate the strategic benefits of partnerships and alliances.

Some of the women from the four organisations participating in this project had had very negative experiences of previous collaboration, believing that their ideas and funding had been 'stolen'. Our initial proposal at the start of the project, that the four NGOs should carry out a joint activity of some kind, was not well received. Each group preferred to work 'privately' on their own internal agenda and issues, and even across the language barriers we were able to detect undercurrents of suspicion, hostility, and a manifest stereotyping of each other's class and politics. There was certainly no automatic commonality of interests.

Gradually, however, as the groups met on a regular basis, they gained confidence in each other, and were able to discuss their parallel processes of organisational learning. They began to discuss problems that they had identified as a result of the consultancy processes. They were able to identify common ground, and have a better understanding of each other. There was less antagonism between them, and they were more open to the idea of co-operation. After several months of meetings, the groups were able to work together on a case-study exercise, concerned with the development of an inter-agency collaboration to address the problem of the trafficking of women. The groups were able to employ the methods and approaches of partnership and inter-agency working that are now common practice in many UK public-sector and voluntary-sector agencies. Although not 'for real', the collaborative exercise evoked strong feelings. However, it helped to identify very vividly the problems that are often encountered in developing collaborative working. The groups were able to recognise that despite *wanting* to work collaboratively, the fear of exposing difference, conflict, and competition between them would prevent collaboration, unless these issues were acknowledged and addressed. They were able to see that these factors had prevented them from achieving collaboration in their own inter-organisational work.

After this constructive experience, we decided to propose to the groups again that they might like to undertake a joint activity, and we proposed that they might collaborate to produce a leaflet. This would inform women about equal rights in Europe, and the implications for Poland if the country joined the EU. The groups were wholly receptive to this proposal.

The groups used the partnership methods that they had learned in the case-study exercise to develop their own collaboration. Together, they examined the strategic purpose of the proposed joint activity, and assessed how working to promote this common purpose would also meet the interests of each organisation. They used a participative planning approach to develop their own proposed joint project. They quickly reached agreement on a project plan and formed a steering group,

composed of two representatives from each organisation, co-ordinated by one member of Women's Rights. This steering group continued to meet after the capacity-building project had been completed, and we left the organisations planning a joint launch of the leaflet on International Women's Day.

By the end of the project, the four NGOs had come to recognise both the purpose of strategic alliances and the necessity of negotiating difference. In the final project evaluation meeting they had this to say:

'We would say that you should look for other organisations that have common interests with yours, and see how you can maximise your impact by working together. Remember that you have to look at problems and issues from different points of view. That diversity of opinion is of value not a problem. Also take into account individual needs and interests within your organisation.'

'Do not be afraid of changes. Do not avoid conflict. We wonder is it conflict that damages the NGO group or is it the avoidance of conflict? We think that finding a common cause raises us above our own individual interests and helps prevent us descending into defending our own view against somebody else. Working on a common activity adds value and makes us stronger.'

Beyond the fragments: developing the longer view

In this article, I have described a capacity-building project which helped women's organisations to confront their own weaknesses. It gave them a range of frameworks and techniques for analysing and solving problems. It also offered a method for managing change, and a language for expressing views and entering into dialogue with one another which transfers the problem away from person-ality, personal rivalries, and hurt, to one focused on issues of strategy, structure, systems, and the stimulus to change.

The four women's organisations which participated in the project now know 'who they are' organisationally, what they like and are good at, and what they are not good at. They are much more aware of how their internal management processes (or lack of them) determine their external impact. The project appears to have helped them to face the reality of the overpopulated NGO terrain in Poland, regarding the challenges of building strategic alliances, in a context in which they face competition for funding. They now have the techniques for project collaboration and inter-agency working.

Whatever the difficulties of the Polish context, it is clearly imperative that women's organisations there should take greater account of their external environment, take time to analyse this, and work on the opportunities that it might provide. When the project started, some of these organisations were neglecting their stakeholders. Subsequently, all of the organisations have become more conscious of their external environment, and the need to continually negotiate and manage the complex and competing interests of their multiple stakeholders.

Yet, on concluding this project, all of us – participants, consultants, and sponsors – were left with a sense of processes just started rather than completed. Only one group had funding beyond the next 12 months, and we left all of the groups locked into short-term work, and facing uncertain futures. There is a convincing argument that all radical and not-for-profit organisations can benefit from being better managed (Landry et al. 1985). However, I would challenge the notion that management systems and rational planning techniques are all that women's organisations require in order to deliver their donors' modernising agenda of strong civil society and democratisation (and somehow, along the way, women's rights). The myth that the mere existence of NGOs, and women's organisations in particular, demonstrates the existence of civil society and women's active citizenship also needs to be challenged. These organisations are struggling.

The discourse of citizenship has re-emerged as a kind of politics for the global age, in which the collectivity of modernity is giving way to more fragmented identities, based on individual rights and responsibilities (Lister 1997). Ruth Lister suggests that if the concept of women's citizenship is to be at all useful for women, it is best understood as a process by which women stake their claim to be included in the construction of civil society and democracy. But this process inevitably involves women's agency and struggle. Poland sharply illustrates that without a responsive and responsible state, women's organisations cannot be effective, and women's citizenship is fairly empty of meaning.

Women's organisations need much more assistance from their sponsors and donors to create the conditions in which they can be effective. This necessarily involves more sustained and on-going capacity building; a different kind of funding regime which helps to develop and promote the longer view; and donors' increased engagement in promoting a public arena based on mutual rights and responsibilities, in which women's organisations can act. Women's organisations do not make civil society – rather, they thrive where a flourishing civil society exists.

Angela Coyle is Professor of Sociology and Director of the Organisation Development Centre at City University, Northampton Square, London EC1V OHB, UK.
a.i.coyle@city.ac.uk

Notes

1   A plenipotentiary is a person or institution invested with the full power of independent action.

References

Biggs, S. and A. Neame (1996) 'Negotiating room for manoeuvre: reflections concerning NGO autonomy and accountability within the new policy agenda' in M. Edwards and D. Hulme (eds.) (1996)

Castells, M. (1998) *End of Millennium*, Oxford: Blackwell

Charles, N. (2000) *Feminism, the State and Social Policy*, Basingstoke: Macmillan Press

Cockburn, C. (2001) *Women Organizing for Change*, Zenica: Medica Zenica u.g., Infoteka

Coyle, A. (2001) 'Women's organisations: high hopes and harsh realities', *The Network Newsletter* 22: 2–3, The British Council www.britishcouncil.org/governance/gendernew/pdf/network22.pdf (last checked by the author 18 November 2003)

DFID (2000) 'Poverty Elimination and the Empowerment of Women', London: Department for International Development

Edwards, M. and D. Hulme (eds.) (1996) *Non-Governmental Organisations – Performance and Accountability: Beyond the Magic Bullet*, London: Earthscan Publications

Einhorn, B. (1991) 'Where have all the women gone? Women and the women's movement in East Central Europe', *Feminist Review* 39: 16-36

Escobar, A. (1995) *Encountering Development: The Making of the Third World*, Princeton: Princeton University Press

Forbes, I. (2002) 'The political meanings of the equal opportunities project' in E. Breitenbach, A. Brown, F. Mackay, and J. Webb (eds.) *The New Politics of Equality in Britain*, Basingstoke and New York: Palgrave

Fuszara, M. (1997) 'Women's movements in Poland' in J.W. Scott, C. Kaplan, and D. Keates (eds.) *Transitions, Environments, Translations*, New York and London: Routledge

Grant, J. (2001) 'Governance, Continuity and Change in the Organised Women's Movement', unpublished doctoral thesis, University of Kent

Gray, J. (1998) *False Dawn*, London: Granta Books

International Helsinki Federation (2000) 'Women 2000: An Investigation into the Status of Women's Rights in the Former Soviet Union and Central and South Eastern Europe', www.ihp.org (last checked by the author February 2002)

Landry, C., D. Morley, R. Southwood, and P. Wright (1985) *What a Way to Run a Railroad: an Analysis of Radical Failure*, London: Comedia Publishing

Lister, R. (1997) *Citizenship: Feminist Perspectives*, Basingstoke: Macmillan Press

Molyneux, M. (1996) 'Women's rights and the international context in the postcommunist states' in M. Threlfall (ed.) *Mapping the Women's Movement*, London and New York: Verso

Pearson, R. and C. Jackson (1998) 'Introduction: Interrogating development: feminism, gender and policy' in C. Jackson and R. Pearson (eds.) *Feminist Visions of Development*, London and New York: Routledge

Stienstra, D. (2000) 'Making global connection among women' in R. Cohen and S. Rai (eds.) *Global Social Movements*, London and New Brunswick: The Athlone Press

Watson, P. (1996) 'The rise of masculinism in Eastern Europe' in M. Threlfall (ed.) *Mapping the Women's Movement*, London and New York: Verso

Wichterich, C. (1998) *The Globalized Woman: Reports from the Future of Inequality*, London and New York: Zed Books

Women's Rights Centre (2000) 'Polish Women in the 1990s' www.free.ngo.pl (last checked by author February 2002)

Gender, citizenship, and nationality in the Arab region

Lina Abou-Habib

Conflict, the need to earn a livelihood, and other factors lead to international migration. Statistics on migration to and from Arab countries are rare, but the existing data shows that the number of women married to foreigners has dramatically increased. This article discusses the work of the Centre for Research and Training on Development in Lebanon, in finding out about investigating discrimination against women citizens married to non-nationals, who are prevented from passing on their nationality to their children. This has a serious impact on the civil, social, economic, and political rights of families in which women have married foreigners.

More than two years ago, my organisation became involved in addressing the issue of women's right to pass on nationality to their children. I work for the Centre for Research and Training on Development (CRTD), a Lebanese non-government organisation (NGO). CRTD has played a key role in setting up a network of organisations in the Arab region (both Maghreb, i.e. North Africa, and Machreq, i.e. the Middle East) within the framework of a regional programme entitled the Machreq/Maghreb Gender Linking and Information Project (MACMAG GLIP).[1]

In early 2001, after MACMAG GLIP identified women's citizenship as an important issue, some work was begun, mainly in Morocco and Lebanon. This consisted of a number of awareness-raising activities (involving dissemination of information, press releases, and placing articles in the local newspapers). In addition we developed training tools and materials (which ended up in a training guidebook on Gender, Citizenship, and Nationality), and began capacity-building activities for local NGOs. We subsequently planned a pan-Arab advocacy campaign.

However, we quickly found that two main issues hindered us. The first was a lack of data on the texts and laws that regulate the issue. We needed not only national data, but data comparing different countries. The second kind of information we needed was hard data on the impact of these laws on women, men, and children. In March 2002, we decided that action research would enable us to investigate these issues and provide women affected by these discriminatory laws with a space to talk about their life experiences and what this discrimination meant for them.

The MACMAG GLIP study

The countries included in the study were Lebanon, Egypt, Syria, Morocco, Tunisia, Yemen, and Jordan. The study was supported by the Gender and Citizenship

Programme of the United Nations Development Programme (UNDP) Programme on Governance in the Arab Region. We focused on gathering information of three main types:

- data on the legal context: national laws and international conventions which have been ratified by the states, relating to the right of women to pass on their nationality to their children
- quantitative data on impact: showing the extent to which the countries of the study are affected
- qualitative data on impact: showing the social, economic, and psychological impacts of this phenomenon on women and their children, as expressed by the women themselves.

Qualitative data were gathered in Lebanon, Egypt, Yemen, Syria, Morocco, and Jordan. Legal information was compiled from all seven countries covered by the study. In each country, legal and administrative data included the Constitution and Nationality Code, administrative and regulative measures relating to the socio-economic and civic rights of the children born of foreign fathers residing in Arab countries, and international conventions ratified by the countries. Socio-demographic data on Arab women married to non-nationals were gathered in Lebanon and Morocco. Detailed qualitative information was gathered on the living conditions of the women affected by the issue, and the impact that their inability to pass on their nationality to their children has on these children's lives. This phase of the research used interviews with ten women per country in Lebanon, Egypt, Syria, Morocco, Tunisia, and Jordan.

The results of the research

International legal bodies and agreements give states the right to set their own regulations regarding the process of granting nationality. They also provide states with the right to specify who their citizens are, according to their independent will and interests. This is because each state is considered to be a separate entity, which has the right to self-rule without interference. Therefore, the ways of granting nationality differ between countries, according to differences between those states' policies, principles, and beliefs.

The national laws

In all seven countries, there is a clear contradiction between the Constitution and the law, regarding the nationality of women and their right to pass it on to their husbands or children. All the Constitutions contain a commitment to gender equity; yet the nationality laws contradict this. Under the law, men have the legal right to pass on their nationality to their non-national spouses and children; whereas women who are married to non-nationals do not have this right, except in a few particular cases[2] – if the child's father is unknown, or if the child's father does not have a nationality.[3] Nationality is inherited through a paternal blood link. Thus, children who have a non-national father cannot inherit the nationality of their home country.

The justification for this discrimination varies between countries. Most countries argue the point on political grounds, considering that giving women the right to pass on their nationality to their husbands and children will threaten the civil peace, and lead to internal political crisis. For example, the state of Lebanon argues that the demographic composition of the country is all-important, and will be destabilised if women married to non-nationals were to grant their nationality to their spouses and children. However, this argument is not used to prevent men giving their nationalities to their non-national wives and children.

National responses to international law

There are many existing international pacts and treaties regarding nationality which aim to eliminate discrimination between men and women, by giving women the right to transfer their nationality to their children. Most of the countries subject to the MACMAG GLIP study had signed at least one, if not several, of these treaties. They include the Nationality Treaty (1930), which first tackled the issue of nationality and urged all the states to regulate this matter. They also include the Universal Declaration of Human Rights (1948); the Convention on the Rights of the Child (1989); the Convention on the Nationality of Married Women (1957); the International Convention on Civil and Political Rights; and the Convention on the Elimination of All Forms of Discrimination against Women – CEDAW – (1979), which identifies in its Article 9 the necessity of 'commitment of member states in providing women equal rights as men in acquiring a nationality, keeping it, or changing it…', and recommends that 'The member states shall provide women equal rights as men in their children's nationality'.

However, the countries which had signed the treaties had mostly done so with reservations. These reservations were deemed necessary because of national policies, legislation, and laws which governments felt clashed with principles enshrined in the treaties. For instance, all the countries covered by the study had ratified CEDAW, with varying degrees of reservation. In many cases, there are so many reservations to CEDAW that these actually hinder the treaty's content and purpose, making it impossible to achieve the Convention's goals.

The extent of the problem

One of the most important objectives of this study was to get an idea of the magnitude of the problem caused by discrimination against women wishing to pass on their citizenship. This would be useful, because it would raise awareness and give political visibility to a social issue that has been concealed. However, the difficulty in obtaining data turned out to be even worse than expected. In practice, we were able to find statistics on the issue in Morocco and Lebanon only. Even here, the information was often incomplete. In Lebanon, the real numbers of mixed marriages are much higher than the available figures suggest, because many foreigners, including those married to Lebanese citizens, fled the country during the civil war. The question of nationality is generally an essentially political question. However, despite these limitations, we decided to present the numbers in our research. They helped us to demystify the issue, and challenge certain prejudices and preconceived ideas.

In Morocco, the project of preparing a general statistical report on marriage and divorce, including mixed marriages, started recently. This is part of a partnership project between the Ministry of Justice and the United Nations Population Fund (UNFPA). During its pilot phase from 1992 to 1996, this initiative led to the creation of a questionnaire on marriages and divorces, to be completed by notaries and returned to the Ministry of Justice, in order to obtain national information on these matters. In 1995 this questionnaire entered general use, but there were problems regarding the reliability of the data obtained (several boxes in the questionnaire often remained empty, or could be incorrectly filled), and national coverage remained patchy, since many tribunals did not send back their questionnaires. However, the data that we obtained in this way remain useful in showing important social trends.

In Morocco over the four-year period, the number of marriages of Moroccan women to non-nationals outnumbered marriages between Moroccan men and foreign women. This result is in itself surprising. Over the four years, such marriages had risen from 996 to 2,507 per year. In 2001, the largest group of foreign husbands were French, who represented 42 per cent of all non-national husbands. Algerians represented only five per cent of foreign men, and men from the 'rest of the Arab World' represented 13 per cent. In the past, the pattern had been that Moroccan women chose foreign husbands who came from countries closer to Morocco, and Algeria in particular.

In Lebanon, in contrast to Morocco, Arabs represented the largest proportion of foreign husbands (61.5 per cent). They were mostly Egyptians (23 per cent), followed by Jordanians (18 per cent), and Iraqis (ten per cent). Meanwhile, Syrians (3.5 per cent) and Palestinians (two per cent) constituted only a small proportion of foreign husbands. Among the non-Arab husbands, the French predominated, representing eight per cent of foreign husbands.

What is the impact on women and their families?

The majority of the women whom we interviewed (62.5 per cent) were still married. Over a quarter (26.8 per cent) were divorced or abandoned, and 10.7 per cent were widows. Marriages tended to have taken place between members of the same religion, except in Morocco, where several Muslim women had married Christian men. Most couples had similar educational levels, but couples who were roughly equal in educational attainment did not usually find equal employment. Some foreign husbands had employment which was superior to that of their wives, but interestingly there were also cases of wives who were in more prestigious professions than their husbands. This is unconventional, and suggests that foreign husbands living in the countries of their wives suffer from the fact that foreign educational qualifications have less prestige in the eyes of employers.

Most women declared that they had chosen their foreign husbands freely, and that most unions were based on love. In Lebanon, some women said they had got married due to 'reason', rather than love, but

still of their own free will. Three women there said they regretted having married too young, saying that they were 'not conscious' at the time. Of the ten Lebanese women to whom we spoke, three had not had their marriages registered with the civil or religious authorities in their husbands' countries. Their children had not been registered, because in one case the father had deserted the home, and, in the other cases, the women did not want Syrian nationality for either their children or themselves. Therefore, their children had no nationality, and their only documents were hospital birth certificates.

Most women reported meeting their husbands through work, studies, family, or friends. In most countries, it took time and effort to reconcile their families to their choice of spouse, but they eventually succeeded. It was harder to get wider social acceptance, however. It was especially hard to gain social approval for spouses who were non-Muslims (even if the woman was Christian), men of a darker skin colour (for example, one respondent was an Egyptian who had married a Ghanaian), and men coming from geographically distant countries. In Egypt, 'traditional' marriages (that is, marriages brokered by the families of the bride and groom) seemed more common, probably because our sample there was older, and these women had come from less privileged social classes. There were also a few 'traditional' marriages in Jordan, which had been organised by families and/or friends. They were generally said to have been instigated in the hope of finding a husband capable of taking care of a divorced woman and her children.

Realising the problem
To what extent had women in our research been conscious of the problems that might arise from marrying a foreigner? In general, most women declared that they had not been warned before marriage. It is clear that women are a long way from knowing the laws that exist in their country, even if they

have a high level of education. The fact that there were no similar cases within women's families or friends meant they had not encountered the issues before. The only thing that most of our respondents were conscious of was that their husbands came from other lands, with other cultures.

In Syria, for instance, most women whom we interviewed thought that the children of an Arab father would automatically have the nationality of their mother. A typical view was: 'When we get married with a Lebanese [because we are both Arabs], we have the impression that we are from the same country'. In Egypt, women condemned the absence of awareness-raising campaigns about the legal problems that they faced as the wives of foreigners, especially given that they thought that the state was primarily responsible for the mixing of people: 'It was during the Union of Syria and Egypt. The two countries were one.'[4]

The refusal by the Registry Office to register the children is generally the harsh first contact with reality. All the women we spoke to had experienced this refusal as a psychological shock, and they felt indignant. Mothers talked of the traumatic experience of going to register their first child, and not being allowed to. Generally, the only way to register the children was to register them with the embassy or consulate of the husband's country. All spoke of this initial sense of shock, and the accompanying feeling of anger and injustice. A typical view was: 'Is it normal that my children, whom I gave birth to, and who were born in Morocco, only have a legal existence in the Algerian Consulate?'

However, registration in the father's consulate could be undertaken only by the father. This was the source of insuperable difficulties when the husband was abroad working, or if there had been a divorce, or if the father had abandoned the family. Other problems arose when the consular services were far away, or when diplomatic relations did not exist, making the issue impossible to solve. These problems were most critical in the case of husbands who were from Arab or developing countries. Women who were married to Westerners did not have the same problems, as their children were automatically registered, and their rights protected.

Judicial and administrative procedures are of diverse types, but it seems that all contribute to make the lives of these families a daily hell. The procedures are extremely complicated, and it is sometimes impossible to renew papers or to pursue divorce settlements in the absence of the father. For families who live in small villages or far from the capital city – that is, the large majority of those to whom we spoke – the procedures that they have to go through, and the investment in time and money that these represent, are costly and hard to bear.

Living with the repercussions

If the husband has died, divorced, or abandoned the home, and children have neither identity papers nor passports, the absence of papers can mean that the whole family lives in fear of police controls. All the countries in our research demand that people carry such documentation. Because of this, the children may feel trapped: as a young Jordanian claimed, 'we are prisoners of our own homes'.

The right to residence

The question of the right to residence is probably one of the most problematic for families in which the wife is national and the husband is foreign. They face the same rules as foreign couples. These procedures are also applied to the children of mixed unions, who reside in the country, after they reach a certain age (for example, 15 in Morocco). If the father's residency permit is cancelled for any reason, the children may have to leave the country with him in order to be able to study and to solve any administrative problems, since, even if he is expelled, he remains their legal tutor.[5] In one case, a woman had to wait two years to enrol her child in school, because her husband was working in another country.

The question of what happens to these families if the husband has to leave is an important point, because, in the Middle East region, countries have in the past suddenly expelled foreigners of countries with whom they were in conflict. For example, during the conflict between Morocco and Algeria, Moroccans have been expelled by Algeria, even when they have ceased to have links with Morocco. Their children, and husbands or wives, have stayed in Algeria.

The right to travel

For mothers and children who do not share the same nationality, problems often arise regarding travel. One woman had had to take her child abroad for more than three months for health reasons. Because the normal maximum time allowed on a return visa is three months, they had suffered incredible difficulties getting the child back into the country.

The right to work

Denial of the right to work was one of the most serious issues facing the families we spoke to. If you are not a citizen of the country, lack of employment places your residence rights in jeopardy. In Syria, if the children of a national mother and foreign father have no work and do not have student status, they cannot stay in the country for longer than three consecutive months.

According to the women whom we interviewed in most countries, husbands and adult children could not work in the public sector. In the private sector there are many rules which make it hard to hire a foreigner. In several countries in our research there is a restriction on foreign Arabs working in either the public or private sector, and in some cases they need an annual working permit. It is often even harder to work in liberal professions. For example, in Syria, foreigners cannot obtain work as doctors.

Having regular work in the country of residence is a fundamental condition for the naturalisation of foreigners. However, work opportunities are often extremely limited for foreigners, leading to a vicious circle: no work without nationality, no nationality without work. Problems with finding employment often drive husbands and children to emigrate or, whenever they can, to work illegally. Illegal work is the source of many difficulties: low pay, precarious terms of employment, and worse. A Jordanian woman married to an Indian national explained what had happened to her husband: 'My husband died because of an accident at work. Since he was not legally allowed to work, his employer refused to pay us the indemnities.'

The right to own property

The right to own property may be forbidden to non-nationals – as in Syria and Lebanon, where couples have to register all property in the name of the woman – and children either cannot inherit or purchase property, or face heavy restrictions. In Tunisia, all foreigners face the same restrictions, regardless of whether or not they are the children of a Tunisian woman.

Access to state aid

In most of the countries covered by the study, when the 'head of the family' is a foreign male, the family is not allowed to benefit from any state aid for under-privileged social classes. In this way, the father's nationality penalises the whole family.

Access to education

In Morocco and Tunisia, the children of national mothers and foreign fathers have no particular problems in accessing primary or secondary education. The story is very different when they reach university, where they face a quota: tertiary education institutions are allowed to admit only a maximum of five per cent foreign students. A mother told us the story of her daughter:

'She has finished her education at the age of 17, two years before she was allowed to get Moroccan nationality. She will not be accepted in any university as a national. She will be part of the five per cent quota of foreigners.' Several mothers hoped that their children would fail their examinations at secondary school, so that they would finish their secondary studies late, at the age of 19. At this age, they could apply for naturalisation. Then they could apply for entrance to university in the same way as nationals.

The impact on marriages

Unsurprisingly, given the number of problems faced by these families, many marriages collapse. As noted earlier, over a quarter of the women to whom we spoke were divorced or had been abandoned.

In most cases, the women who took part in our research declared that if they had to take the decision to marry a foreigner today, they would not do it. They showed anger against the state and laws which deny women citizens the same rights as men: 'I do not understand why it is easier for the foreign wife of a Moroccan man to obtain the [Moroccan] nationality, than for the foreign husband of a Moroccan woman. I am also a citizen, I work, and I pay taxes.'

Women were also angry at being forced by discriminatory laws to challenge gender norms, which placed them at odds with society. There is a great feeling of contradiction, as the woman has to bear a lot of what would normally be the husband's responsibilities. The dependence of women on their husbands is a value which is central to the societies in which our respondents live. One woman told us: 'I feel that I am living a great contradiction, that comes from an inversion in our roles. I take my husband's role now because, since he cannot work, I have to support everyone.' Women who support their husbands face heavy social sanctions. They do not want to appear as what in fact they feel themselves to be: diminished women with diminished husbands.

Because of the need to keep up appearances, women often felt that they had to face the consequences of their choice alone. They felt extremely lonely because of this. Many admitted that they did not ask for help from their families, feeling that they had to bear the consequences of their choice with dignity and pride. In fact, several of the interviewed women declared that they did everything they could to project the image of a 'perfect couple'. If a couple is unhappy, women can be subjected to constant fear and blackmail, since their husbands can leave at any time with their children, who generally appear on their father's passport. This was a daily worry for some women we spoke to, who had had to accept the unacceptable in order to keep their children.

The interviewed women reported often feeling guilty, and they often regretted their decision. They felt guilty towards their children: 'I am the reason why my daughters have no future'. Their regret at having married a foreigner was made worse by their feelings of humiliation and shame. An Egyptian woman summarised this: 'As a wife, I have known love, but as a mother I have lost my children for ever, and I do not advise any woman to marry a foreigner.'

To sum up, all the women felt that the situation was unfair: a violation of the rights and dignity of women, and of the principles of equality and citizenship. However, the nature of their problems, and the severity of them, varied greatly. Those married to Arabs, Africans, or people from other developing countries had suffered much more, both financially and socially. Families with low incomes were also more affected by the injustice of the situation. On the other hand, women who had married Westerners found that they had a certain number of advantages, and their marriages were more socially acceptable. This is a strange and paradoxical result, since the marriage of a Muslim to a non-Muslim is generally less accepted socially. However, the norms are modified by economic reality, and it seems that the financial advantages that marriage to a

European is likely to bring can outweigh the problem of initial family rejection.

Children are considered foreigners, despite the fact that they have lived in their mother's native country all their lives. The question of identity seems to be especially important for the children. One Lebanese mother talked of her son, who persistently asks: 'Why am I not Lebanese?'. The overwhelming message was that the children of a foreign father feel that they miss out on benefits that other children have. They resent being different, and they are generally very sensitive to prejudices and negative judgements. One mother stated, 'My son has hung a Moroccan flag in his bedroom. It's his way of claiming his nationality.'

Strategies used by the women to solve their problems

One key distinction divided the women into two groups. The first group consisted of those married to Western men. They had found that their situation gave them advantages which outweighed the denial of their right to pass on their nationality and citizenship to their children. As the worst problem that they faced, this group mentioned the psychological impact of the situation on their children. The second group was those married to Arabs, Africans, or other nationals from developing countries. They felt that they were disadvantaged overall and suffered because of their situation, and were likely to try actively to challenge it. Despite the knowledge that their actions may be fruitless, ('my position is weak because the laws are against me'), most of the women made repeated and multiple efforts.

However, despite these differences, the strategies that women used to cope with their situation were fairly similar.

Individual strategies

Challenging the law directly

Women used their right to a judicial appeal, by filing complaints at a tribunal. They consulted lawyers; the lawyer of one woman who tried this advised her not to do anything, as it would all be in vain. The women complained and petitioned for residence rights for the children, and for children to feature on the mother's passport.

Circumventing the law

Women had lobbied government ministers to obtain nationality for the children, and enlisted help from influential people. Some had used false papers to register the children in schools, hospitals, and to obtain social security. Most women who had done this had resorted to their social network to get advice and obtain papers. These networks also proved to be useful in giving their husbands bank guarantees, which are required to get a work permit. Finally, they would register the property of their husbands and children in the mother's name.

Collective strategies

Very few women had tried resorting to collective action through involvement with the work of NGOs, except in Lebanon, Morocco, and Tunisia, where there were small and very specific examples of work on the issue.

Conclusion

This regional research has revealed facts and figures about an issue which has been so far neglected. All the women whom we interviewed felt that the fact that they were not able to pass on nationality and citizenship to their children was a deprivation of a fundamental right. This action discriminates against women in two ways:

- as individuals, by restricting their right to live as full citizens with the husband of their choice;

- as mothers, since they are deprived of the right to transmit their nationality, and the citizenship rights that this confers, to their children.

In addition, children are discriminated against because they are born, grow up, play, and study in a country that refuses to recognise them as human beings who have full and equal citizenship rights in the country of their birth; and because they live with a mother who is incapable, according to the law, of guaranteeing them a normal life, and such elementary rights as the rights to travel, to study, or to work.

The following recommendations are the result of the research project, and represent the thinking of the women to whom we spoke.

Long-term objectives

The main objective in most countries is to develop an appropriate social policy, including the assertion of women's rights, under the Constitution, to transmit their nationality to their children (regardless of the father's attitude); recognition of the importance of preserving the unity of the family; and acknowledging women's citizenship in terms of rights and duties.

Other (often related) long-term objectives include:

- equal treatment for foreign wives and foreign husbands in the naturalisation process;

- equality of rights to higher education and employment for children of all bi-national couples;

- right of children to obtain the nationality of the country in which they were born, regardless of their parents' nationalities (in Tunisia).

Short-term recommendations

- Women who want to marry foreigners must be informed of the laws on nationality and citizenship, and of the consequences for their children's rights.

- Women should be allowed to register children on their mother's passport regardless of their citizenship.

- The requirement for residence permits for children of foreign fathers should be abolished.

- Children should be naturalised at the age of 15.

- Permits for residence and work permits should be made more accessible, financially as well as in terms of procedures.

- The status of 'permanent resident' should be given to children who have resided for more than five years in the country

- Mothers should be given permission to be the legal tutors of their children.

- Associations of women affected by these issues should be established.

- Women affected by these issues should have the right to make collective appeals at Constitutional Court level.

- NGOs should be made aware of the issues, so that they can advocate for changes to be made to laws, Nationality Codes, and Personal Status Codes.

At present, we are disseminating the information generated by the study, in the form of articles, publications, press releases, and meetings with the media. Women affected by these discriminatory laws are being encouraged to form collective interest groups. Finally, proposals for legal reforms are under way. These will be primarily based on the findings of the research. In addition, in early October 2003, a regional meeting was organised in collaboration with UNDP Programme of Governance in the Arab Region (POGAR). Parliament and media representatives from the seven countries of the study were invited to discuss the findings and implications of the research, in an effort to build alliances as well as a collective plan of action for change.

Lina Abou-Habib is the Co-ordinator of The Centre for Research and Training on Development (CRTD) and of the Machreq/ Maghreb Gender Linking and Information Project (MACMAG GLIP). Address: CRTD, POB 165302, Achrafieh 1100 2030, Beirut, Lebanon.
labouhabib@macmag-glip.org

Notes

1 The organisations in MACMAG GLIP are NGO Forum for Women in Development in Egypt; Association Démocratique des Femmes au Maroc in Morocco; Queen Zein Charaf Institute for Development (ZENID) in Jordan; the Syrian Women League in Syria; the Civic Democratic Initiative in Yemen; and CRTD in Lebanon.

2 In the case of divorce or death of the father, women may resort to a court appeal requesting that their children under 18 be granted nationality if they live in their mother's country. This however is a lengthy and costly procedure, and success is not guaranteed. Women will have to be literate, well resourced, and well connected to use the law.

3 Moreover, in most of the countries in this study, these two cases apply only if the child was born in his or her mother's homeland.

4 Syria and Egypt were in a Union from 1958 to 1961.

5 Because fathers are the recognised heads of household, they are the legal tutors of their minor children, even if the mother is the provider.

Deprived of an individual identity:
citizenship and women in Nepal

Mona Laczo[1]

Development organisations aiming to end violence against women, and to promote women's empowerment in societies such as Nepal, need to pay attention to the question of women's citizenship, and its links to empowerment and independence. In Nepal, citizenship rights are still accorded to women through male relatives, rather than in their own right. Many women are unaware of the importance of citizenship; yet others associate citizenship with an independent identity, the freedom to make choices, and the ability to obtain education, a good job, and a future. This article, by a development worker, identifies the barriers to women's citizenship that exist in Nepal, and focuses on the additional obstacles to citizenship faced by ethnic minorities, trafficked women and children, and refugees. Currently, organisations based in Nepal are working in alliance with international development agencies to call for reforms enabling women to gain full and equal citizenship with men.

This article discusses citizenship in Nepal, women's attitudes to the denial of full citizenship rights, and its impact on equality between women and men. Citizenship is a basic human right in our world of nation states. Citizenship is a direct link between an individual and the state in which he or she lives. Through it, the state and the individual have mutual responsibility towards each other. The state has the responsibility to provide for its citizens, and the citizen has the responsibility to defend the sovereignty of the state. Citizenship legitimises people's access to public resources and allows their participation in public life. Yet millions of people are deprived of this relationship with the state, and this has a devastating impact on their daily lives. The largest category of people who are affected by discrimination regarding citizenship rights is women.

After he stepped on the top of the world's highest mountain, Mount Everest, some 50 years ago, Sir Edmund Hillary was granted honorary citizenship of Nepal, backed up by the Constitution of Nepal itself. Yet thousands of Nepali women lack citizenship rights. Some are poor, some rich, some uneducated, some educated, some from villages, and some from cities. This article explores the reasons for this deprivation, and its impact. It draws on interviews conducted by me in the course of my work with Oxfam GB as Regional Media and Advocacy Co-ordinator for South Asia. I have been fascinated by this issue for the past five years, and have spoken to many people in the course of visits to refugee camps, to areas where Oxfam GB supports development work, and in my personal travels.

Women and citizenship in Nepal

'If I could have citizenship without my father or my husband, I would have an identity that belongs only to me.'
(A trafficking survivor, research interview)

The right to citizenship is safeguarded by a

number of human-rights conventions, including the Universal Declaration of Human Rights. A number of key international instruments specifically address the issue of citizenship and statelessness. Article 15 of the Universal Declaration of Human Rights states that '1. Everyone has the right to a nationality. 2. No one shall be arbitrarily deprived of his nationality nor denied the right to change his nationality'. The Convention on the Elimination of All Forms of Discrimination against Women (CEDAW) clearly states that states should grant citizenship rights to its citizens, regardless of gender. '1. State Parties shall grant women equal rights with men to acquire, change or retain their nationality. They shall ensure in particular that neither marriage to an alien nor change of nationality by the husband during marriage shall automatically change the nationality of the wife, render her stateless or force upon her the nationality of her husband' (CEDAW Article 9). Paragraph 2 of Article 9 further defines the issue of inheritance of nationality. It states that 'States Parties shall grant women equal rights with men with respect to the nationality of their children'.

Nepal is party to 16 international conventions, including CEDAW. However, it has at least 118 legal provisions, including the Constitution, that discriminate against women (Forum for Women, Law, and Development 2000). These include inheritance laws, marriage laws, and the law on citizenship. In all these areas, women's rights are bestowed on them by virtue of their relationship to their fathers, brothers, or husbands. As Sapana Pradhan Malla, a Supreme Court Advocate in Nepal, notes: 'the discriminatory laws against women pose a major hurdle in the road to achieving gender equality' (*The Kathmandu Post*, 19 January 2003).

Barriers to citizenship in Nepal

Citizenship in Nepal is gendered, in the sense that women and men have different and unequal access to it. This is due to various legal provisions and principles, including the Constitution of Nepal (1990). Citizenship is awarded on blood rights – that is, fathers pass citizenship to their sons and daughters. After the age of 16, both men and women must apply for a Certificate of Citizenship, to ensure that their citizenship rights are protected. However, while this process is relatively straightforward for a young man, it is not so for a woman, whose application must be supported by either her father or her husband. This deepens women's dependence on male relatives, and renders them more vulnerable to discrimination and violence within the family.

Thousands more Nepalese women are denied rights of citizenship because they have been trafficked against their will, or they belong to ethnic minorities, or they are refugees. While all these women's rights to gain citizenship are being violated, the nature of the violations differs from case to case. For example, most survivors of trafficking are ostracised or socially excluded by their communities and families, and their fathers are reluctant to acknowledge their existence. Further barriers to citizenship are faced by women – and men – from some ethnic minority groups. For refugee women rendered stateless, the question is even bigger, because there is no effective body to guarantee their status.

Minority ethnic groups may face particular problems in gaining citizenship. This is despite the fact that Nepal is a country that prides itself on its diverse ethnic fabric, and its laws prohibit discrimination based on religion, sex, ethnicity, and so on. Article 11.2 of the Constitution states that 'No discrimination shall be made against any citizen in the application of general laws on grounds of religion (*dharma*), race (*varya*), sex (*liga*), caste (*jat*), tribe (*jati*), or ideological conviction (*varicarik*) or any of these'. Paragraph 3 of the same article goes further, stipulating that the state should not practise discrimination among its citizens. Yet, despite a clear legal framework to limit discrimination against ethnic groups, in practice such discrimination does occur. For example, officials in charge of issuing identification documents, such as birth certificates or citizenship cards, can make every attempt to hinder the already burdensome bureaucratic process, which at the end discourages ethnic communities from applying (personal communication, August 2002).

A final group which faces problems consists of the children and spouses of mixed marriages between Nepalese women and foreign nationals. Women and men whose fathers are not Nepalese are denied Nepalese citizenship. The Constitution of 1990 and the Citizenship Act of 1963 state that women cannot transfer their citizenship to their children or spouses. The Country Code of 1963, paragraph 152.1, provides for the recognition of a person as having inherited Nepalese citizenship through the father, but not through the mother. Questions 5-10 on the forms for the Certificate of Citizenship relate only to an applicant's father's and husband's details – including citizenship – but no similar details can be noted on the mother's or wife's side. This leaves women without a chance to pass their citizenship to their children or their foreign husbands directly.

The process of application

'The current system of identification of women through their husband violates women's human rights.'
(Personal communication, Yam Bahadur Kisan, Oxfam Legal Consultant, 19 June 2003, Pokhara, Nepal)

While some might argue that getting citizenship in Nepal is not impossible, most say that the bureaucratic process in place, along with numerous legal discriminatory provisions, makes it difficult and burdensome for women to apply.

In order to apply for citizenship, you have to provide evidence that your birth has been registered. The process of registering a birth, and later applying for citizenship, is entangled in a number of bureaucratic procedures. The process could be made easier if birth registration was seen by all as a custom and a necessary process. However, according to UNICEF, only about 21 per cent of births are registered in Nepal, and these are mostly in major towns. 'In Nepal people don't believe that registering the birth of their children can bring benefit in their lives, but birth certificates could play a vital role in a child's life. It can define their access to higher education, government employment, voting, or even contesting in an election' (personal communication, Yam Bahadur Kisan, Oxfam Legal Consultant, 20 July 2003).

Tellingly, the directions for the photograph needed for the Nepalese Citizenship Certificate Application Form are tailored to men. The form says 'black and white photo must show both ears wearing a Nepali traditional hat'. Only men wear such a hat.

Some women to whom I spoke reported that they had asked the authorities for citizenship papers and had been rejected. Others reported that it had taken them years to secure their citizenship papers, as the authorities continued to harass them for more paperwork. Many women told me that the pressures of daily life prevented them from taking the initiative to apply for their papers.

There is low awareness on the part of many women about the process. For example, one of the women whom I met in the course of my research for this article described her fear of losing her citizenship, because her husband, who had applied for it, had suddenly left her for another woman: 'Now, I really don't know what to do. I would like to ask my father to get me a citizenship certificate, but he told me to go back to my husband. But why should I go back to a husband who beat me up, and who doesn't treat me well?' (personal communication, 19 June 2003, Pokhara, Nepal). Yet the belief that she would lose her citizenship just because her husband had left her is simply wrong.

The impact of lack of citizenship

The extent of the problems caused by lack of citizenship is not fully known in Nepal, as studies have not been conducted on the issue, but the problems are without doubt extremely serious. Women – and men – who are without citizenship have no legal identity. This means that they may not be able to pursue legal suits if their rights in law are violated. Women's current widespread lack of access to citizenship limits their options in every aspect of life, be it access to education, health services, or freedom of movement. In rural areas of Nepal, it is the norm for people to have limited information about their legal rights to citizenship, and little understanding of how citizenship could contribute to their independence and empowerment.

However, some women to whom I spoke have realised that citizenship potentially means power to break out of poverty and build a better future, through ensuring that women are able to gain access to public resources. Women told me they felt that without citizenship a woman is nothing, as she is always at the mercy of her father, her brother, and her husband. A girl learns early on that her status within the family will be less than that of her brothers. She will leave the family house as soon as she is deemed ready for marriage. This depends not on having reached a particular age, but on her father's subjective judgement. Without

citizenship, a woman is stuck in the village, and is more likely to be trapped in the vicious cycle of violence.

In an interview, Meena, a young woman from an ethnic minority, stated: 'Citizenship is very important in life, without it you are nothing. It is an evidence that proves my identity. It can get you a job, it can get you an education. I have a citizenship card, that is why I can work. Most women who are without it are left in the village with no possibility of a brighter future. Everywhere you go, people ask you about your citizenship. At checkpoints, at health clinics, at schools everywhere… and not everybody can prove that they have it' (personal communication, 19 June 2003, Pokhara, Nepal).

In the remainder of this section, I look briefly at two particular groups within the wider population of Nepal, and outline the impact that lack of access to citizenship has on them.

Trafficked women and children

'My brother and uncle sold me to traffickers. Luckily I was rescued. But now I am told that these very people will have to help me with my request for a citizenship card. How could this be fair?'
(A survivor of trafficking)

It is estimated that more than 600,000 girls and young women are 'missing' from Nepal. They are victims of one of the most heinous crimes in today's world: human trafficking. Many of them have been trafficked to neighbouring countries such as India, where they are forced to work as sex workers in big cities, like Mumbai. Many of those who are trafficked lack citizenship. They are either too young to have received it before they were trafficked, or their parents never initiated the application process.

Citizenship can also act as a tool in the fight against trafficking of women and children. One of the reasons why it is so easy to traffic thousands of children out of Nepal is that they often come from poor families and are not registered by their parents, and thus there is very little trace of their existence. Once they are trafficked, women and children can find it difficult to prove their nationality, which can prolong their difficulties in being returned to their home countries. Many survivors of trafficking are faced with the dilemma of not being able to prove their place of origin and as a result could be subjected to further violence, not only by those who trafficked them but also by authorities who are supposed to protect them. There are numerous well-documented reports of girls being sold and resold – even by policemen, who feel little remorse about the practice.

Shakti Samuha, a small membership organisation in Nepal, works with survivors of trafficking. One of its objectives is to ensure the promotion of citizenship for women in Nepal, because it sees a direct link between trafficking and the lack of citizenship documents. If a woman with formal rights of citizenship is trafficked, people can actually find out where she is from and help to facilitate her return. If she is lost, there is a chance for the family to find her by means of the documents.

At the recent South Asia Court of Women on the Violence of Trafficking and HIV/AIDS, jurors heard evidence that citizenship can actually help trafficked women and children to regain their identity and facilitate their return. Bhagawati Nepal's testimony to the jury included the following: 'The victim is socially ostracised. She is not allowed to participate in any of the religious ceremonies. The family does not accept her because they fear society would boycott them as well. Since the victims do not have citizenship they are not given employment. Since the survivor is not left with any option, she often takes up prostitution or in extreme cases, commits suicide' (personal court testimony, South Asia Court of Women on the Violence of Trafficking and HIV/AIDS, 11 August 2003, Dhaka, Bangladesh).

Refugees

Perhaps no other group of women is more disadvantaged than the Bhutanese refugee women living in Nepal. These women have been stripped (along with their whole families) of their Bhutanese citizenship, and are now living in refugee camps and urban centres in Nepal, rendered 'stateless'. For such women, citizenship is a fantasy: 'There is no such a thing as being a global citizen. If there was, I could claim it and could receive a passport and could travel everywhere. I could send my children to school without fear that our status would be found out. I could open a bank account to save my money for the future. I could buy a house on a little plot of land. If there was such a thing as global citizenship, I could live without fear' (interview, Bhutanese refugee living in Nepal, 23 June 2003).

The Bhutanese refugee crisis started in the late 1970s, when the then conservative Bhutanese government 'introduced a series of … discriminatory measures focused on the political, economic and cultural expulsion of Nepali-speakers' (Human Rights Watch 2003). The crisis escalated in 1991, when the Bhutanese government rendered more than 100,000 of its Nepali-origin citizens 'non-citizens'. This figure represents one-sixth of the population of this small kingdom. By 1991, the government's stance resulted in the forced expulsion of thousands of people. 'I never thought that citizenship is an important thing, until I was told by the only government I knew that I was no longer considered a citizen. At that point I realised that I was rendered a nobody,' a refugee woman from Bhutan told me in an interview.

Many legal advocates state that the Bhutanese government's attempt to strip people of their citizenship runs counter to the call of the United Nations to reduce the incidence of statelessness. An Amnesty International Report on the issue states the following: 'The provisions of Bhutan's nationality law, which provide for the removal of nationality or which deem that people leaving the country have renounced their nationality without making such loss of nationality contingent on acquisition of another nationality, run counter to these principles. Neither Nepal nor India normally permit dual citizenship, so Bhutanese of Nepal ethnic origin originating from either of those countries who acquired Bhutanese citizenship would have had to relinquish their formal citizenship' (Amnesty International 2000, no page number).

Some of the women leaders of the Bhutanese refugees now living in Nepal talk of the dilemmas they face as a result of losing their citizenship. As one woman leader recounted, 'Women need to have a safe environment, because they are always thinking about their families. But how could we think about providing the best for our families, when we don't even have an identity either here in Nepal or in Bhutan?' (personal communication, 24 July 2003, Kathmandu, Nepal).

These women leaders also worry about the fate of the new generation of Bhutanese refugees who are now coming of age. 'Citizenship cannot be indoctrinated, as it has to be in one's blood. You should have a feeling towards your country as your country gives its duties to you and you give your duties to the country. But how could the new generation understand this, when their country had told them that it doesn't want them?' (personal communication, 24 July 2003, Kathmandu, Nepal).

Conclusions

Citizenship is gendered in Nepal in favour of men, leaving women vulnerable and without an individual identity. Equal access to citizenship would go a long way towards helping women to acquire an individual identity, beyond their roles as wives, sisters, daughters, and mothers. This would be an important step in the fight for equal rights of women within the family, the community, and the Nepalese state as a whole. It would

enable women to build their own individual identities and lives.

While most women in Nepal do not fully understand the benefits of citizenship, some of those who do understand have started a movement to ensure that constitutional change will bring about equality and betterment of women's lives. A number of local civil-society groups are already working on the issue of ensuring women's rights in various legal provisions. One such agency is the Forum of Women, Law, and Development; another is Shakti Samuha, an organisation consisting of, and working with, survivors of trafficking. However, much more is needed to bring the issue to the attention of the policy makers and bring about change. Non-government organisations and groups from civil society have a great role to play in promoting the citizenship rights of women in Nepal and in actually bringing about social change.

However, while a lot of work so far has been done to highlight the problem of gender discrimination in the citizenship laws in Nepal – such as identifying legal provisions that discriminate against women and advocating for change in the law – real change has not come yet. Most of the work so far has been done by organisations working to promote legal rights and human rights. There is a great need for a more diverse group of organisations to come together and discuss and tackle the issue. These should include women's groups in the villages, educators, policy makers, representatives of civil society, and donors.

Mona Laczo is the Regional Media and Advocacy Co-ordinator for Oxfam GB in South Asia. She has an MA in Asia Pacific Studies from the University of San Francisco. Her interest in citizenship issues comes from her personal experiences, as well as her work with immigrants, asylum seekers, and refugees in the USA, and South and Southeast Asia. Address: Oxfam GB, House #4, Road #3, Banani, Dhaka 1213, Bangladesh.
mlaczo@oxfam.org.uk

Notes

1 I would like to thank my colleagues on the Oxfam team in Nepal, especially Sandhya Shrestha, who have all been keen to help me with this work, and continue to discuss and seek answers to this very important issue.

References

Amnesty International (2000) 'Nationality, Expulsion, Statelessness and the Right to Return', www.amnesty.org (last checked by the author September 2003)

Forum for Women, Law, and Development (2000) 'Discriminatory Laws in Nepal and Their Impact on Women: A Review of the Current Situation and Proposals for Change', www.fwld.org.np/dl.html (last checked by the editor 26 November 2003)

Human Rights Watch (2003) 'We Don't Want to Be Refugees Again', Briefing Paper for the Fourteenth Ministerial Joint Committee of Bhutan and Nepal, 19 May 2003

The Kathmandu Post (2003) 'When citizens without citizenship certificate speak out', 19 January 2003

Women and citizenship in global teacher education:
the Global-ITE Project

Jayashree Inbaraj, Subbalakshmi Kumar, Hellen Sambili, and Alison Scott-Baumann

The Global-ITE (Initial Teacher Education) scheme is a three-year education project. It aims to enable trainee teachers in three teacher-education institutes in India, Kenya, and England to link local and global social issues to each other, and relate them to the school curriculum; and to promote a global perspective on citizenship education. Integral to our vision of global citizenship is gender equality, together with a respect for diversity. The project leaders in each country are women academics, as is the project adviser, and there is a preponderance of women students involved in the project. This gives women a voice in a vitally important area of international curriculum development. However, there are outstanding questions to be resolved about the limits on women's ability to influence change beyond the project, when men still make many operational and resourcing decisions in world politics.

The term citizenship has many inter-pretations. All over the world, even in countries with democratic govern-ments and wealthy economies, there is disillusionment for many citizens across all categories of age, race, and social class, who perceive huge discrepancies between democratic ideals and reality. Global citizen-ship education aims to render children able to cope with social, economic, and political changes, which will affect them in many ways. It also aims to make them socially and environmentally 'competent' – that is, able to effect change in the world in which they live. The development of moral sensibility depends on our believing in our own ability to make a difference through our actions. Students may perceive injustice regarding the environment, civil rights, and the systems that influence their lives, yet they may not be aware that they have the ability to influence these matters.

Currently, there is much debate in India, England, and Kenya about citizenship education, and immense scepticism about the contents of any civic education programme. In India, citizenship education is new (Kumar 2003). Some feel that a govern-ment body, under political pressure, has started pandering to narrow partisan views, biasing textbooks to conform to the Hindutva ideology (associated with Hindu nationalism), and introducing citizenship education. In Kenya, there are many differences of opinion about citizenship (often divided along ethnic lines), and 'the recent introduction of multiparty democracy has polarised further the ethnic divide and introduced another element of conflict – political conflict' (Maritim 2003, 2), in the context of Africa.

In England, the Crick Report was commissioned by the current government, and was published in 1998. It launched a four-year preparation period for teaching citizenship in schools. Some in England are suspicious about the Labour government's motive for introducing a citizenship programme: is this out of a desire for a biddable electorate rather than activist citizens, and is either of these compatible with democratic ideals? (Scott-Baumann, 2003a). The Crick Report has been influential in the debate about citizenship. It admits that there is no clear agreement on the definition of citizenship, but describes it as including 'the nature and practices of participation in democracy; the duties, responsibilities and rights of individuals as citizens; and the value to individuals and society of community activity' (QCA 1998, 4). The writers of the Crick Report emphasise the importance of political literacy, and encourage community activity and active learning in the course of learning specific subjects. There is some mention of multicultural work in the report, but little emphasis on global citizenship.

We can understand the scepticism about the nature and scope of citizenship education, and why it is introduced in particular political contexts. We also recognise the discrepancies between textbook messages about citizenship, and actual experiences in particular societies. Such variations give people every reason to be wary of new endeavours such as our own. At the moment in India, no teacher is expected to defend or promote citizenship education, either in schools or in teacher education colleges. In England, legislation now requires every school to teach citizenship, but there is considerable resistance from the teachers, who feel ill-equipped to teach a subject – with a disputed content and teaching methods – that may include controversial topics. In Kenya, the long-term influence of the recent fundamental power shifts in government is not yet apparent.

The Global-ITE project will therefore need to keep abreast of developments in, and attitudes to, citizenship education within each country. An additional challenge for the project is the current lack of consensus on the definition and scope of what citizenship education would include. Whose ideals are we developing in such a project? Education for global citizenship deserves a strong endorsement if it is understood as being about exposing people to world issues, and views of the world, which promote justice and equity.

Global citizenship and gender equality

The issue of gender equality is a key element in our own understanding of global citizenship. Teaching global citizenship does not only require teachers to possess the qualities of technical proficiency in a subject, and efficient communication skills. They also need to understand issues of social justice as problems associated with class, gender, ethnicity, internationalism, drug taking, violence or environmentalism, with which contemporary society is profoundly concerned.

We, the four women academics writing this article, hope that the Global-ITE team is united in the cause of helping girls and women to become more than 'a means to other people's welfare and well-being' (Mitter 2001, 40). We believe that projects like this should affirm universal values. Yet our shared belief systems are a complex combination of spiritual and secular influences – incorporating Hinduism, a commitment to human rights, African Christianity, and European philosophy with a Protestant flavour (as seen in the work of Ricoeur). We find it is often difficult to clarify what these universal values are that we share, particularly with regard to women's rights. Alison Scott-Baumann has worked on developing teacher education for Muslim women in England; this work showed the importance of not assuming that individual women's personal choices will be consonant with Western feminism, or even international feminism (Scott-Baumann, 2003b).

We think that clarifying our vision of women's rights depends on committing ourselves to debate, plurality of vision, and a capacity to admit uncertainty. Teachers who educate children to be global citizens also need to base their teaching methods on these commitments. The Global-ITE project hopes to create opportunities for women educationalists from different cultures to meet and discuss the concept of global citizenship with each other; understand themselves and each other better; and develop some shared understanding of women's rights. All over the world, social policy, including education policy, is based on different views of gender relations, based on world views and value systems which conflict with each other.

For example, in Kenya, the Social Ethics Education (SEE) programme is taught as part of the national curriculum and asserts that it promotes the modernisation of society – by, for example, endorsing the nuclear rather than the extended family, and promoting marriage relationships in which final authority for decision making rests with the husband. This is at odds with the ethos of the Centres for Excellence Schools for Rescued Girls in Kenya, which provide an educational programme for our student teachers on the global programme. The Centres for Excellence act as refuges for girls rescued before female genital mutilation (FGM) and early marriage, and may therefore challenge this authority of the male head of household. Reconciliation is attempted with their families, since this work is perceived as a direct challenge to traditional patriarchy. Such schools also support families who reject their rescued daughters, and attempt to bridge the gulf between old ways and new.

In India, a 'reservation system' allocates a percentage of educational places to those of lower caste. This is now seen by many as discriminatory and undemocratic. Yet new legislation is planned to increase reserved places for women in the job market, in the same way that places in education and employment have been reserved for decades for *dalit* ('Untouchable') men and women, and this gives rise to considerable debate.

A final example, from England, is the citizenship education programme that is being developed for schools. In terms of gender awareness, this is based on the unspoken assumption that European girls and women can freely choose to lead the life they wish. This should, but does not, lead to debate about the truth of this assumption, and also about whether girls and women really use the choices they are accredited with, to benefit themselves and others.

These examples show how complex the issues are. Building a commitment to gender equality into the Global-ITE programme will require assertive action in all three countries. This cannot come solely from educationalists – it must involve the women's movement. In Kenya, there are strong women's movements, but their goals may be different from the national school programme of SEE. In India there are texts used in schools that refer to the status of women and their role in politics and give the mistaken impression that women in India have real influence. This could be clarified and perhaps changed by working with women's organisations. In England it seems that the notion of consumer choice gives girls (and boys) the impression or illusion that they have freedom to develop their full potential to find solutions to world poverty, and the other issues that citizens of the world must be responsible for: this requires attention within the citizenship curriculum.

The next section of the article outlines the structure of the Global-ITE project, in order to contextualise the gender-related work that plays an integral part in it.

The Global-ITE project

The institutional bedrock for Global-ITE in each country is the teacher-education programme at each of three universities (Mumbai in India, Egerton in Kenya, and Gloucestershire in England). The project is co-ordinated by a UK-based non-government organisation (NGO), Global Dimensions, and funded by the Department for International Development (DFID).

The intended aims of the project are as follows:

- to develop a global perspective, including understanding of other cultures and our responsibilities towards each other. It incorporates studies on peace, equality, values and perceptions, human rights, conflict resolution, interdependence, social justice, sustainability and citizenship, and will be fully integrated into the curriculum of the teacher education programmes in all three countries

- to teach teachers (in both universities and schools) and pupils to understand the local and global injustices that result from unfair distribution of wealth, education, healthcare and resources

- to help teachers and pupils to develop some solutions that they can act upon, such as Fair Trade activities and campaigns to inform the community about unfair practices

- to incorporate a global dimension into the taught curriculum, enriching subjects such as geography, history, religious studies, mathematics, science, business studies, and art

- to provide key staff with appropriate resources (in terms of time, space, and equipment), to support the development of the global perspective on citizenship education across the curriculum

- to make relevant teacher development opportunities available for all educators involved in the Global ITE project at the three institutions, including working with NGOs.

An integral part of the project is inter-regional visits: these take place annually and include an international conference, run each year by one of the partner institutions. There are other forms of interaction between the host institutions, including website development, creation and use of global teaching materials, and e-mail communication to develop ideas collaboratively. The people involved are student teachers, teacher trainers, school head-teachers, and university academics from each country.

In order to meet the aims above, we believe that we need to assist teachers to reflect critically on their own attitudes and practice. In the project, we are helping them to do this by adopting an approach to global citizenship that is based on development-education principles. This approach aims to raise awareness of learners' own preconceptions and beliefs, and make their assumptions explicit. The following case studies show different ways in which this process can take place. Each of the case studies focuses on gender issues.

Case study from India: issues of equality

The hypothesis, based on anecdotal evidence, was that school textbooks in India are often based on material which depicts traditional occupations for women and men. The idea that these roles are natural rather than socially constructed is unconsciously instilled in the minds of the children, and left unquestioned because of the status of the teaching material. During the pilot project for the Global-ITE programme in 2000, a student teacher at Kapila Khandvala College of Teacher Education in Mumbai, called Sandesh Kadam, analysed a Standard Ten Maharashtra State Syllabus science textbook (for 15-16 year olds) (Kadam 2000). Sandesh wanted to see whether the science textbook reflected gender bias.

There were five objectives to the study:

- to analyse the sex and occupation of particular people in the textbook, and how bias is transmitted in language and narrative;

- to analyse sex, socio-economic level, occupation, and type of activity of people appearing in the illustrations and photographs;

- to seek examples in the textbook that imply women do unimportant, low-status work;

- to suggest changes for the revision of the textbook, to remove gender stereotypes which lead to discrimination against women;

- to sensitise students to the existence of gender stereotyping, and the reasons why this is detrimental to the cause of gender equality.

Data were analysed by focusing on the language, narrative, and the illustrations in the textbook. Analysis of the male-female ratio of the editorial working committee that wrote the textbook showed that all members of the working committee were male.

It became clear to the pupils in Sandesh's class that illustrations, pictures, and the language used perpetuate traditional role typing. On the basis of the findings, this student teacher, working as a researcher, made concrete recommendations for necessary revision in the science textbook to reflect gender sensitivity. Subsequently, classroom activities were developed to sensitise children to gender issues. The teacher asked students to draw non-discriminatory pictures.

In another example, Prabha Arora, an Indian Global-ITE trainee teacher in 2002-3, carried out a project to reduce gender stereotypes (Arora 2003). Her study included simple exercises such as asking students to draw a domestic scene in their house at 7 p.m. In a class of 50, most students drew a picture of the mother in the kitchen and the father reading a newspaper. (A description of the project is available at www.global-ite.org.) The trainee teacher designed interesting exercises to sensitise children about their own stereotyped attitudes and beliefs.

Jayashree Inbaraj's experience as project co-ordinator for Global-ITE in Mumbai shows her that teachers can do a good job, provided that they are given intensive training and also are convinced about its importance. She notices that many trainee teachers feel that a focus on gender inequality is outdated. They believe that gender studies are less relevant and less important in our fast-changing world than

media studies or pressing environmental problems. They need convincing that gender inequality is still a highly significant issue. It is true that the teacher-education curriculum all over India shows concern for gender discrimination. Equality is in the syllabus. The core elements of the National Education Policy (1986) give emphasis to gender equality. However, in a short course of one year, in which the student is grappling with the basics of classroom pedagogy, the importance of such issues gets lost. Even if there is awareness of the issue in the trainee, there may be little knowledge about how to translate these concerns into day-to-day teaching. For instance, a trainee teacher may mention that boys and girls should be treated equally in a general way, but may make no attempt to move beyond this statement.

The Global-ITE project helps to develop motivation and teaching approaches for gender work by educating pre-service teachers to bring in a global dimension to their teaching. The eight key concepts that are emphasised are peace, interdependence, equality, values and perceptions, human rights, citizenship, conflict resolution, and social justice. The teacher takes up issues to deal with in the classroom that relate to any of the key concepts.

Using the key concepts from the Global-ITE project as a starting point, trainees in Mumbai have incorporated gender equality in their day-to-day teaching through different subjects. For example, using statistics in mathematics and civics to explain why there is a 30 per cent reservation of seats for women in the Indian Parliament. The teacher then needs to work sensitively on the fact that statistics may not reveal the whole truth. For instance, in the rural villages of India, more women are involved in governance, since the 30 per cent reservation, known as a quota system, was introduced for women. Consequently, many women now hold the post of *Sarpanch* (head of the *panchayat*, the local government body), but actual decisions are taken by men. Women are easily manipulated, coerced, and co-opted by their male counterparts. Also, styles of dress, election campaign meetings, and strategies for women are often still decided by the male members of the family. Despite this there is agreement among women activists that the first step is to help women to enter politics, and then their awareness of their potential to act will rise. The *panchayati raj* institutions are to be valued as the real nurseries of political leadership for women. Women can fight discrimination and bring about change if they form a critical mass in decision-making bodies, from village *panchayat* to parliament. Anecdotal evidence of this is building up. The teacher who is sensitive to these issues, as a result of taking part in the Global-ITE programme, can provide more facts for his or her pupils from a broader perspective.

Case study from Kenya: the power of narrative

In Kenya, rural women with no education are twice as likely to be in poverty as those who have attended school, and more than half the girls in Kenya are not enrolled in school (Lalai, 2002). One of the purposes of the project in Kenya is to provide examples of experiences of real women to support this statistic.

Scholastica Kinyanjui, a Kenyan Global-ITE trainee teacher in 2002-3, developed an action research project on conflict resolution in a farming community (Kinyanjui 2003). She developed lesson plans to cover facts about crops, and also to help her pupils to debate and resolve conflict. She established a clear, contextualised human-rights agenda as the basis for her teaching, here set out in her own words:

Human Rights
Women and children are the people who work to earn family income.
A lot of idleness is demonstrated by men, who spend time lying and chatting at the shopping
centres while the women are working on the farms.
Excessive drinking by men from the rural communities is at the expense of needs of other family members.
There should be an equal distribution of family resources.
More children need access to education opportunities (education should be the right of all persons).
Improve health as a result of better nutrition through learning about a balanced diet in the Global-ITE project.

A major strength of the Kenyan approach to global citizenship education lies in the use of drama. On Global-ITE visits, schools and the university use performances that depict the reality of life for many Kenyan women, with dramatic narrative. These performances portray the solutions that Kenyan girls and women are developing, in order to make a life for themselves that is within their control. The themes that recur, in all the Kenyan presentations and plays that focus on girls and women, are at the very core of womanhood. They deal with issues ranging from the rights of ownership of one's body, to freedom from violation and pain, to human reproductive choice, and to independence of spirit.

Hellen Sambili feels that there is growing evidence that the Global-ITE project has made some impact in the host schools and their surrounding communities, and will do more in future. The students perform skits during parents' days, prize-giving days, and fundraising days – focusing on such issues as the devastation caused to families by AIDS deaths. The dramas 'persuade' the adults to ponder the real issues, and – we hope – determine to do something to improve the quality of life for themselves and their community. Global-ITE clubs have started in some schools, meeting once a week to discuss topics informally, including the negative and inhuman effects of FGM, and the denial of educational opportunities for the girl child. A female drama teacher at Kericho, a boys' school, taught a pupil, Eugene Maritim, to recite a solo verse ('Feel/Talk for your sister') on the problems that girls face when they come from communities that still practise FGM. This was performed to the whole school during a visit by the English team of researchers and student teachers. Some girls and boys have been invited to perform during Global-ITE workshops attended by over a dozen school head-teachers, teacher educators, and student teachers.

At the Centre of Excellence School for Girls in Kajiado, the girls acted out the preparations of the elders for a Masai girl's circumcision. The drama depicted the pubescent girl's mother's belief that this is the right and appropriate course of action, and the girl's subsequent escape from FGM and early marriage, via the Centre's rescue programme. Another girls' school, run by nuns, acted out a play that the girls wrote and directed themselves, in which a young woman who desperately needs a job is preyed upon for sexual favours by her boss, and contracts HIV, leading to AIDS. The girls and their teachers planned to tour local schools with their play, as a consciousness-raising activity. A third performance took place at the university, where student teachers depicted the drunken, abusive behaviour of a husband towards his wife. The wife eventually sought support from a woman friend to give her the strength to resist such treatment.

These performances are of exceptionally high standard in terms of their capacity to increase our understanding through pity and through terror, and through the occasional use of comedy, reminding us of how human we all are. For the Global-ITE visitors there are discussions with educators about the subject matter of the plays. There is also another reason for the potency of the plays that were originally created for the Global-ITE visitors; Kenyans often say of themselves that they are both ignorant and modest in the way in which they talk about

sexual matters, and would prefer to avoid the subject. Thus, teaching honestly about HIV/AIDS is difficult, as certain key words may not even exist in Kikuyu or Kiswahili (Tombo 2002). These plays facilitate understanding without forcing discussion.

Some approaches are less subtle: the Kenyan Youth Education and Community Development Programme (KYEDCP), based in Nairobi, is an NGO funded and run by Kenyans. It runs uncharacteristically 'tough-talking' courses for young Kenyans. One of the founders of KYECDP and its national director are both women, and they act as role models for the Global-ITE visitors. This seems particularly significant in terms of understanding that women have the ability to take action; and in a world where many of our actions are carried out for us by machines, the belief that we can make a difference is itself empowering. This NGO provides part of the education programme for Global-ITE teachers, presenting an understanding of urban dilemmas in Nairobi.

Case study from England: the benefits of visits to India and Kenya

The work of Annie Coskun, a trainee geography teacher and Global-ITE student in 2002-3, shows the benefit of visits for trainee teachers, and how usefully this can inform the development of global awareness in England (Coskun 2003). Annie sees herself as a citizen of the world and, as a result of her involvement with the project, uses a great deal of global citizenship material in her geography teaching. In her own words:

'One outcome that really comes to mind is the work I can do now, as a geography teacher, on water use. I made a video in Kenya of several boys collecting water in oil barrels, using a donkey and cart. They were running their own enterprise, selling the water. Their efforts to collect it really

made the kids over here think about how much water they use. I use this video for teaching. I now do a starter activity about how much water you use to clean your teeth, asking the children to put the plug in the basin and measure water use. Here, in Gloucestershire, my pupils are shocked by how much water they waste.'

Annie wishes to continue to work with the project by linking a school in Kenya with a school in Swindon. She is working closely with a head-teacher, John Kirui, to plan curriculum links. She would also like to involve the Swindon pupils in fundraising, as John Kirui's school needs a wind pump to draw up more and cleaner water for the pupils.

Annie's work is subject-specific, and this is true of much of the work currently undertaken by the English Global-ITE group. The National Curriculum and the assessment-focused agendas of the English secondary-school system constrain the opportunities for teaching about citizenship, belying its potential as an empowering, knowledge-giving subject. A deeper debate, using a more issues-based approach – where an issue like poverty or gender takes precedence over the formal requirements of the curriculum – is desirable.

Conclusions: women as pawns or players in global citizenship?

In school placements in all three countries, our Global-ITE trainee teachers have often been faced with lack of support from the schools in which they learn to teach. More clarity is needed to understand and express personal belief systems (Newell Jones 2003). Each Global-ITE student teacher has similar yet differing global priorities – for example, some will be more interested in working on women's issues, some on helping children, some on improving water supplies – and these personal differences will be rooted in each person's belief system. Above all, the belief systems of each key worker must be allowed to permeate the development work that they incorporate into their teaching, so that commitment can be developed.

It is hoped that this project can help the trainee teachers to look beyond their local context to a bigger, shared horizon, where they see themselves reflected in others, and try to understand others better. For example, the rights on which the Global-ITE work in Kenya focuses are taken for granted by many European women, yet trafficking, bonded sex and domestic work, domestic violence, and other violations of these rights exist nonetheless in Europe.

If we refuse to take risks within the curriculum, at both university and school levels, then we will remain pawns, unable to implement change. If significant long-term impact is to be achieved by the Global-ITE project, it will be necessary to work together to be strong players in global education. We need to consolidate the work achieved by the past students of this project; providing in-service training, developing teaching materials that can be made widely available, and continuing to develop electronic communication, such as the current website. Moreover there is work like Philosophy for Children[1] which may help us to develop communities of enquiry in the classroom.

We can also learn from our Indian colleagues, who have been working in this way for longer. They recommend the issues-based approach, in which an issue such as gender equality is developed as the prime focus within the subject teaching of the national curriculum. The tendency in secondary education in England is to adhere to the subjects in the curriculum and insert a little global understanding (with the subject remaining the main focus). The issues-based approach would help us to teach a topic such as gender and development in greater depth, because the issue is seen as more important than the curriculum requirements of a geography course that deals, for example, with tourism in Kenya for a few lessons.

It is also vital to work with both governmental and educational agencies, in a way that will facilitate sustainable development of the global dimension in education, with schools and universities taking responsibility for developing fully integrated global citizenship education programmes.

Jayashree Inbaraj is a teacher educator at Kapila Khandvala College of Teacher Education at the University of Mumbai, India. She has worked in development education for the past 15 years. Address: C-11, Shantijeevan Nivas, Vidyanagari, Mumbai, 400098, India.
jayai@vsnl.com

Subbalakshmi Kumar is an experienced educational consultant, with a special interest in development education, dating back 15 years. She advises the British Council on school linking and other projects. Address: D2/3, Ratan Park – Phase 11, Pashan Sus Rd, Pune, 411021, India.
subhakumar@vsnl.com

Professor Hellen Sambili is a scientist with particular interest in agriculture and in development education, and manages international exchange programmes at Egerton University. Address: Egerton University, Nguro Campus, Kenya.
teriki@swiftkenya.com

Dr Alison Scott-Baumann is a teacher educator, psychologist, and philosopher who manages several ethics programmes, including global citizenship. Address: School of Education, University of Gloucestershire, Francis Close Hall, Swindon Road, Cheltenham, Glos, GL50 4AZ, UK.
asbaumann@glos.ac.uk

Notes

1 Philosophy for Children works on global citizenship and developing a teaching and learning framework to help teachers to become facilitators of debate, while embodying moral authority and facilitating ethical decision making in children. Philosophy for Children provides training to establish an atmosphere of trust in which controversial issues can be discussed and belief systems can be developed and articulated. For more information, see www. sapere.net and www.aude-education.co.uk.

References

Arora, P. (2003) 'Action Research Project: Eliminating Stereotypes – Developing an Objective Attitude', Mumbai: University of Mumbai

Coskun, A. (2003) 'Action Research Project: Water Conservation', Cheltenham: University of Gloucestershire

Kadam, S. (2000) 'Action Research Project: A Critical Analysis of the Science Textbook (Maharashtra State Syllabus) for Gender Bias', Mumbai: University of Mumbai

Kinyanjui, S. (2003) 'Action Research Project: Farming, Conflict Resolution and Health', Egerton: Egerton University

Kumar, S. (2003) 'Education for an Enduring Society', Global Citizenship conference paper, Cheltenham: University of Gloucestershire

Lalai, V. (2002) 'Working with Africa', Global Citizenship conference paper, Egerton: University of Egerton

Maritim, E.K. (2003) 'Education for All in Africa', Global Citizenship conference paper, Cheltenham: University of Gloucestershire

Mitter, S. (2001) 'Universalism's struggle', *Radical Philosophy* 108: 40-2

Newell Jones, K. (2003) 'Developing Global Understanding', workshop materials for

Global-ITE students, Cheltenham: University of Gloucestershire

QCA (1998) *Education for Citizenship and the Teaching of Democracy in Schools* (The Crick Report), London: Qualifications and Curriculum Authority

Ricoeur, P. (1986) *Fallible Man* (translation C. Kelbley, introduction W. Lowe), New York: Fordham University Press (first published as *L'Homme faillible*, 1960)

Ricoeur, P. (1992) *Oneself as Another* (translation K. Blamey), Chicago: University of Chicago Press (first published as *Soi-même comme un autre*, 1990)

Scott-Baumann, A. (2003a) 'Citizenship and postmodernity', *Intercultural Education* (forthcoming, December 2003)

Scott-Baumann, A. (2003b) 'Teacher education for Muslim women', *Ethnicities* 3(2): 243-61

Tombo, H. (2002) 'Kenyan Youth Education and Community Development: Programme Sensitisation Talk', workshop for Global-ITE students, Nairobi

Resources

Compiled by Lina Abou-Habib with Erin Leigh

Publications

Women, Citizenship and Difference (1999) Pnina Werbner and Nira Yuval-Davis (eds.), Zed Books, 7 Cynthia Street, London N1 9JF / Room 400, 175 Fifth Avenue, New York, NY 100010, USA.
www.zedbooks.demon.co.uk

This companion to the *Feminist Review* special issue (see Journals below) is based on a conference held in 1996 entitled 'Women, Citizenship, and Difference'. It considers citizenship for women and men, and how these gender identities are also shaped by other factors, such as race, class, ethnicity, and national status. It offers a mix of both country-based and more general analysis. The theoretical approach makes it a challenging read, but this is an important and classic text.

Feminism and Citizenship (1998) Rian Voet, Sage Publications, 6 Bonhill Street, London EC2A 4PU, UK.
www.sagepub.com

The author presents an original reflection on key issues related to citizenship, and argues for gender equality to be incorporated into the understanding and analysis of citizenship. The book challenges the view that gender equality and citizenship are different areas of interest and concern, and instead insists that they should be integrated. Not an easy read, but an important publication nevertheless.

Citizenship: Feminist Perspectives (2nd edition 2003) Ruth Lister, Palgrave Macmillan, Houndmills, Basingstoke, Hampshire, UK RG21 6XS / 175 Fifth Avenue, New York, NY 10010, USA.
www.palgrave.com

Lister presents a feminist critique of mainstream understandings of citizenship. A consideration of the social-policy context, and especially the private/public divide, is integrated into the theoretical analysis.

Toward a Feminist Theory of the State (1991) Catharine A. Mackinnon, Harvard University Press, Fitzroy House, 11 Chenies Street, London WC1E 7EY, UK / Harvard University Press, 79 Garden Street, Cambridge, Massachusetts 02138, USA.
www.hup.harvard.edu

After analysing women's subordinate status in relationship to men, the author then considers this relationship with respect to the state. The volume presents an informed and compelling critique of inequality, and a transformative vision for social change.

Policy, Politics and Gender (1998) Kathleen Staudt, Kumarian Press, 14 Oakwood Avenue, West Hartford, Connecticut 06119-2127, USA.
www.kpbooks.com

Staudt analyses women's exclusion from democratic processes, and national and international government departments.

Women's exclusion from bureaucracies, and the shortcomings of 'women's offices' in government are addressed. Staudt shows how the unsustainability and over-consumption of state policies and development schemes is linked to their exclusion of women from planning and practice, and she offers strategies for mainstreaming gender into government institutions and policies.

Beyond Equality and Difference: Citizenship, Feminist Politics, Female Subjectivity (1992) Gisela Bock and Susan James (eds.), Routledge, 11 New Fetter Lane, London EC4P 4EE, UK.
www.routledge.com

This book, based on a conference held in 1988, examines the use of the terms 'equality' and 'difference' in feminist approaches. It argues that the current definitions are based on 'male' criteria, and presents new definitions that are women-centred.

Young People at the Centre: Participation and Social Change (2001) Jane Foster and Kumi Naidoo (eds.), CIVICUS and Commonwealth Secretariat, Information and Public Affairs Division, Commonwealth Secretariat, Marlborough House, Pall Mall, London SW1Y 5HX, UK.
r.jones-parry@commonwealth.int

Young People at the Centre makes an important contribution to the sparse literature on youth and development. At its core is a recognition of young people's contributions to society through active citizenship. Gender equality is highlighted throughout as an important factor to consider in youth participation, and is addressed in some of the case studies and personal profiles. Ten brief case studies and nine profiles of people active on youth-related issues are featured, demonstrating the capacities and varied nature of concerned youth from around the world. These are supported by chapters that set the context of youth participation, and how it is demonstrated at the macro, meso, and micro levels. The book ends with a useful list of further resources.

Multicultural Jurisdictions: Cultural Differences and Women's Rights (2001) Ayelet Shachar, Cambridge University Press, The Edinburgh Building, Cambridge CB2 2RU, UK / 40 West 20th Street, New York, NY 10011-4211, USA / Dock House, The Waterfront, Cape Town 8001, South Africa.
http://uk.cambridge.org/

The author considers multicultural understandings of citizenship that include the notion of the rights of 'minority' groups, as opposed to the rights of individuals. She argues that the dominant ways of governing in a multicultural society require a person to choose between his or her tradition/culture, and his or her status as an individual. Using the example of family law, and its particular impacts on women, she demonstrates that giving too much power to minority groups could permit violations of the rights of their individual members, particularly women. She proposes a method of 'joint governance' between the state and minority groups to overcome the polarised approaches and allow individuals to retain both their cultural identity and their individual rights.

Women 2000 and Beyond: Women, Nationality and Citizenship (2003) UN Division for the Advancement of Women (DAW).
English copies available at:
www.un.org/womenwatch/daw/public/june03e.pdf
Spanish copies available at:
www.un.org/womenwatch/daw/public/june03s.pdf
daw@un.org
This text examines laws that differentiate between women and men in the acquisition and retention of nationality, as well as in relation to the nationality of their children.

Subversive Women: Women's Movements in Africa, Asia, Latin America and the Caribbean (1995) Saskia Wieringa (ed.), Kali for Women and Zed Books, Kali for Women, K-92, 1st Floor, Hauz Khas Enclave, New Delhi 110 016, India.
www.kalibooks.com

Historical analyses of women's movements from around the world are presented here. Defying the myth that feminism is a solely Western construct and export, the book describes multiple forms of women's resistance in Peru, Sudan, Somalia, Indonesia, India, and the Caribbean. The result of a research project undertaken by the Institute of Social Studies (ISS), the book includes an honest reflection on the research process in the chapter 'Methods and Power: Epistemological and Methodological Aspects of a Feminist Research Project'. Although the publication dates from 1995, the historical content is relevant today.

The Space Between Us: Negotiating Gender and National Identities in Conflict (1998) Cynthia Cockburn, Zed Books, 7 Cynthia Street, London N1 9JF / Room 400, 175 Fifth Avenue, New York, NY 100010, USA.
www.zedbooks.demon.co.uk

This study focuses on three well-known conflict zones: Northern Ireland, Israel/Palestine, and Bosnia-Herzegovina. After an introductory chapter on women and nationalism in these three areas, Cockburn examines each area separately. She provides a brief historical background for each of the conflicts, and discusses the roles that women have been playing in them. Finally, she analyses three women's organisations working for peace: the Women's Network in Belfast, Bat Shalom in Israel, and Medical Women's Therapy Centre in Bosnia-Herzegovina.

Women, Ethnicity and Nationalism (1998) Rick Wilford and Robert L. Miller (eds.), Routledge, 11 New Fetter Lane, London EC4P 4EE, UK.
www.routledge.com

This collection analyses the relationships between gender equality, nationalism, and traditional movements. The contributors explore how women's roles have been changed, or shaped, by national struggles, ethnic conflict, foreign occupation, and civil war. That 'liberation' of the nation does not equal 'liberation of women' is clearly demonstrated. Essays on the following countries are included: Northern Ireland, South Africa, Russia and the former Yugoslavia, Yemen, Lebanon, and Malaysia.

Women, Islam and the State (1991) Deniz Kandiyoti (ed.), Temple University Press, 1601 N. Broad Street, 306 USB, Philadelphia PA 19122, USA.
www.temple.edu/tempress

Taking a historical-comparative approach, Kandiyoti selects articles that examine a range of conditions for women in Islamic societies in contemporary Middle Eastern and South Asian countries. Essentially the book adopts a gender perspective in order to analyse state transformation and its effect on Muslim societies. Case studies are drawn from Turkey, Iran, Pakistan, Bangladesh, India, Iraq, Lebanon, Egypt, and Yemen.

Governing for Equity: Gender, Citizenship and Governance (2003) Maitrayee Mukhopadhyay (ed.), Royal Tropical Institute (KIT), KIT Publishers, PO Box 95001, 1090 HA Amsterdam, The Netherlands.
www.kit.nl

Governing for Equity brings together the findings from KIT's three-year research programme 'Gender, Citizenship, and Governance', and a conference entitled 'Governing for Equity' (2002). The publication reports on some of the conference proceedings, including keynote speeches by Gita Sen and Pregs Govender, and presents insider insights on working on gender and governance in various institutions. including the World Bank and UNICEF. It then summarises the work of its various action research projects in Southern Africa and South Asia (see a related article by Mukhopadhyay in this issue for more information). Finally, discussions from the conference are included, as are conclusions and a synthesis of key concepts, including good governance and citizenship. Their website also provides useful information and resources on gender and governance.

No Shortcuts to Power: African Women in Politics and Policy Making (2003) Anne Marie Goetz and Shireen Hassim (eds.), Zed Books, 7 Cynthia Street, London N1 9JF / Room 400, 175 Fifth Avenue, New York, NY 100010, USA.
www.zedbooks.demon.co.uk

This book considers women's access, presence, and influence in politics, drawing on a comparative analysis of conditions in Uganda and South Africa. Both these countries have made good progress towards equal political representation for women, and so provide valuable case studies with relevance beyond their borders. The contributors analyse the characteristics of the state and civil society that enable women's participation in politics, and discuss to what extent their presence in politics facilitates the promotion of gender equality in policy and legislation. Chapter 2 presents a useful framework for assessing whether women's representation in the state and civil society is likely to lead to meaningful advances towards gender equality, rather than to a mere increase in the numbers of women in politics. The framework identifies different structures of accountability as a necessary means to support gender equality.

Women's Movements in International Perspective: Latin America and Beyond (2001) Maxine Molyneux, Palgrave Macmillan, Houndmills, Basingstoke, Hampshire, UK RG21 6XS / 175 Fifth Avenue, New York, NY 10010, USA.
www.palgrave.com

Molyneux examines women's movements in Latin America, including case studies from Argentina, Nicaragua, and Cuba. Of particular relevance is a chapter entitled 'Analysing Women's Movements', which presents a framework for understanding women's movements depending on the level of their independence from other movements and politics, and whether or not they are informed by specifically women's interests, or are composed of women. She proposes a distinction between practical and strategic interests, nuancing the debate that has been simplified over time. Also of interest is her chapter on gender and citizenship on the continent from a historical perspective. From the initial theoretical analysis, an ensuing discussion illustrates ways in which women's claims to citizenship rights have been shaped by active participation in civil society. In addition, the gendered nature of such citizenship is shown to be initially reliant on differences between women and men, and on women's traditional roles as mothers and carers.

Gender and Citizenship in the Middle East (2000) Suad Joseph (ed.), Syracuse University Press, Syracuse, New York 13244-5160, USA.
http://sumweb.syr.edu/su_press

Beginning with an abstract but thoughtful introduction, this work is organised into four sections, dealing with North Africa, Eastern Arab States, The Arab Gulf, and the non-Arab Middle East. Less theoretical than the introduction, country-specific essays examine the ways in which Arab women are excluded from the rights that are characteristic of 'full citizens'. The history behind concepts of 'citizenship' in the Middle East, and their relevance, is questioned. Major recurring themes include the influence of religion on citizenship; the importance of the family, not the individual, as the most basic unit of the state; and family law.

Colonial Citizens (2000) Elizabeth Thompson, Columbia University Press, 136 S. Broadway, Irvington, NY 10533, USA.
www.columbia.edu/cu/cup

This work offers the fullest English account of Syrian and Lebanese women's history to date, and examines 'civic order' in French-mandated Lebanon and Syria. Thompson argues that the colonial civic order both carried gender inequalities within it and encouraged gender hierarchies. This colonial civic order thus framed the concept of citizenship with the understanding that gender relations are unequal. This concept of unequal citizenship continues to affect Lebanon and Syria today.

In the Eye of the Storm: Women in Post-Revolutionary Iran (1994) Mahnaz Afkhami and Erika Friedl (eds.), I.B. Tauris, 45 Bloomsbury Square, London WC1A 2HY, UK. www.ibtauris.com

In the Eye of the Storm illustrates how the legal and cultural environment in post-revolutionary Iran has greatly affected the ways in which women participate in, and benefit from, their family, society, and state. Particularly useful to those interested in citizenship rights are the appendices that focus on the 'Legal Status of Women in the Family in Iran' and 'Islamic Penal Code of the Islamic Republic of Iran'.

Feminists, Islam and Nation: Gender and the Making of Modern Egypt (1995) Margot Badran, Princeton University Press, 41 William Street, Princeton, New Jersey 08540, USA.
http://pup.princeton.edu/

Badran tells the little-known story of Egyptian feminism and the decisive role that it played in the creation of the modern Egyptian state.

Women of a Non-State Nation: The Kurds (2001) Shahrzad Mojab (ed.), Mazda Publishers, PO Box 2603, Costa Meso, California 92626, USA. www.mazdapub.com

Contributors examine aspects of Kurdish women's lives in politics, history, culture, religion, medicine, and language. Some topics have never appeared in previous studies: gender and self-determination, women and Sufism, language and patriarchy, and women in traditional medicine. The first section on historical perspectives is of particular relevance to a study of citizenship.

Women in Kuwait (1993) Haya al-Mughni, Saqi Books, 26 Westbourne Grove, London W2 5RH, UK.
www.saqibooks.com

Haya al-Mughni shows how a series of historical, economic, and political events have shaped the development of Kuwaiti women. The oil era, the growth of the state, the emergence of women's organisations, and the Islamic revival are examined in terms of their impact on women's status and identity.

Rethinking Modernity and National Identity in Turkey (1997) Sibel Bozdogan and Resat Kasaba (eds.), University of Washington Press, Marketing Dept., PO Box 50096, Seattle, WA 98145-5096, USA.
www.washington.edu/uwpress

Mainly drawing on the proceedings of an international conference entitled 'Re-thinking the Project of Modernity in Turkey', the editors present critical analyses of modernisation and its effect on Turkey culturally, socially, and politically. Two chapters of the book focus on the relationship between gender and modernity. The first considers the emergence of feminists critical of modernisation, but maintaining a middle ground between Islamic feminists and Kemalists. The second discusses the formulation of the modern family and the construction of gender under modernisation.

Journals

Feminist Review, Palgrave Macmillan, Houndmills, Basingstoke, Hampshire, UK RG21 6XS / 175 Fifth Avenue, New York, NY 10010, USA.
www.palgrave-journals.com/fr/index.html
www.feminist-review.com

Feminist Review published a special issue in 1997 (no. 57, Autumn) entitled 'Citizenship: Pushing the Boundaries'. This review aims to give its reader a glimpse into the issues relating to 'gender and citizenship' around the world. The contributions include Women, Citizenship and Difference; Gender, Disability and Citizenship in Australia; The Lebanese Case; Fortress Europe; Foreign Domestic Workers in Canada; and Women's Publics and the Search for New Democracies.

Training manuals and briefing papers

A Training Manual for Grassroots Organisations: Understanding Gender and Citizenship (2003) Centre for Research and Training on Development (CRTD), POB 165302, 1100 2030 Beirut, Lebanon.
info@crtd.org
www.crtd.org

The CRTD manual, written for development practitioners and activists, aims to provide skills, information, and illustrations for conducting participatory training on gender and citizenship.

Association for Women's Rights in Development (AWID) Facts and Issues, Women's Rights and Economic Change; Nos.1 and 2 August (2002) Alison Symington, AWID, 96 Spadina Ave., Suite 401, Toronto, ON, Canada M5V 2J6.
Available online at
www.awid.org/publications/primers/factsissues
mwigglesworth@awid.org

The first two primers available in this series are useful for prompting thinking about rights-based approaches to gender and development. The first, *A Rights-Based Approach to Development,* provides an accessible introduction with a gender perspective. The second, *The Convention on the Elimination of All Forms of Discrimination Against Women and the Optional Protocol,* discusses how to use this international convention on women's rights both in judicial initiatives and as a resource for planning advocacy and lobbying work. The entire series is available in French and Spanish, as well as English.

Circle of Rights: Economic, Social and Cultural Rights Activism: A Training Resource (2000) International Human Rights Internship Program (IHRIP) and Asian Forum for Human Rights and Development (Forum-Asia), IHRIP, Institute of Education (IIE), 1400 K Street, N.W., Suite 650, Washington DC 20005, USA.
ihrip@iie.org

Forum-Asia, 109 Suthisarnwinichai Road, Samsennok, Huaykwang, Bangkok 10320, Thailand.
forumasiabkk@mozart.inet.co.th

This thorough training resource provides an introduction to economic, social, and cultural rights. An introduction to a rights-based perspective is followed by the historical development of such rights. Each module is prefaced with a clear outline of its purpose. There is an important section on different groups' concerns and relationship to such rights, including women, children, indigenous peoples, and refugees. Gender perspectives on the rights to work, to own land and property, and to access health services are included in the section on women, as well as a history of women's rights as human rights. *Circle of Rights* also presents strategies and tools for activism at both the national and regional levels.

Electronic resources

BRIDGE, Institute of Development Studies, University of Sussex, UK.
bridge@ids.ac.uk
www.ids.ac.uk/bridge/

Established in 1992, BRIDGE is now an established non-profit-making unit specialising in gender and development, based at the Institute of Development Studies in the UK. Information resources and papers are on their website. In addition, available in print and electronically are their Cutting Edge packs, which include Internet materials, BRIDGE bibliographies, Gender and Development in Brief (BRIDGE bulletins), and BRIDGE glossaries. Gender and Citizenship is a forthcoming theme. BRIDGE also hosts two resources websites – Siyanda and Genie – to facilitate the sharing of information and materials on gender and development.

'Women in Contemporary Democratization' (2000) Shahra Razavi, Occasional Paper No. 4, Geneva: UNRISD
www.unrisd.org

Razavi begins with the question of how to reform democratic institutions to be more gender-equitable – especially given the extremely low levels of women's participation in formal politics. The paper consists of three main sections, which include an analysis of women's movements and the role they played in bringing about democracy; how women have tried to achieve change by joining political processes or influencing them from the outside; and whether or not women should engage with political institutions, or remain independent of them. Razavi argues that it is necessary to have strong women's movements outside of government, to help to ensure that gender mainstreaming is not just a technical exercise, and to apply pressure for meaningful change. Case studies include Brazil, Chile, Cuba, Uganda, and South Africa.

Women's Political Participation and Good Governance: 21st Century Challenges (2000) UNDP
http://magnet.undp.org/new/pdf/gender/wpp/women_book.pdf

This online book contains very useful information on gender and governance with a general overview of the concepts, in-depth case studies, and overall conclusions. Included among the case studies are an analysis of India's local-government quotas for women; the gender budget in South Africa; Uganda's women's caucus; and campaigns to end violence against women in Latin America and the Caribbean.

UNDP Gender in Development Programme: Monograph Series
www.sdnp.undp.org/gender/resources/monograph.html

This series includes important papers on gender and urban governance (Jo Beall), and 'Gendered governance: an agenda for change' (Georgina Ashworth). They argue that current systems of governance privilege men over women, and that there is a need to make them gender-sensitive. In addition,

there is a paper on the *Panchayat Raj* system of quotas for women's participation in local governance in India (Devaki Jain).

Gender and Citizenship Initiative – UNDP POGAR
pogar@pogar.org
www.undp-pogar.org

In partnership with the International Development Research Centre (IDRC) in Canada, the UNDP Bureau for Arab States' Regional Governance Programme (UNDP POGAR) launched in December 2001 the Gender and Citizenship Initiative, aiming to encourage policy debates and dialogue on women's citizenship in selected Arab countries; raise awareness of gender inequalities in legislation; build the capacity of Arab women's NGOs to lobby for policy changes; and build partnerships between women's NGOs and parliamentarians.

Women Are Citizens Too: The Laws of the State, the Lives of Women (2002) Nadia Hijab, Regional Bureau for Arab States, UNDP
www.undppogar.org/publications/gender/nadia/summary.pdf

Nadia Hijab presents a synthesis of four Gender and Citizenship papers discussed at a meeting of experts co-organised by UNDP and Maroc 20/20 in Casablanca, later presented in Amman. The papers consider family laws, social protection laws, nationality, and election laws and their impact on the relationship between women and citizenship in the Arab states.

Websites

Inter-Parliamentary Union – Women in Politics
www.ipu.org/iss-e/women.htm

The Inter-Parliamentary Union (IPU) works to advance women's participation in parliaments. Its website discusses women's presence in the IPU; provides a bibliographic database of publications relating to women and politics; and presents statistical data and country-by-country comparisons of the degree to which women are represented in parliaments.

Women's Human Rights Resources
www.law-lib.utoronto.ca/Diana
whrr.law@utoronto.ca

This website provides information and resources on international human rights for women. It contains a searchable database of articles, publications, and papers, provided with thorough abstracts. Many of these resources are available through the site. The site also offers advocacy guides, research guides, and special features.

Cool Planet
www.oxfam.org.uk/coolplanet/teachers/globciti/index.htm

Part of Oxfam GB's Development Education programme, this website is a useful resource for teachers of children and young people. 'Global Citizenship' as a component of education is promoted on the site, which suggests how children can learn to live their lives by considering the world around them from the perspective of social justice, and how this can be included in formal education. The suggested curriculum for UK-based teachers could be relevant for a broader group of formal and non-formal youth educators in both the North and South.

Organisations

Women's Learning Partnership for Rights, Development, and Peace (WLP), 4343 Montgomery Avenue, Suite 201, Bethesda MD 20814, USA. Tel: +1 301 654 2774; Fax: +1 301 654 2775
wlp@learningpartnership.org;
www.learningpartnership.org

Women's Learning Partnership for Rights, Development, and Peace (WLP) is an international, non-government organisation which empowers women and girls in the global South to re-imagine and re-structure their roles in their families, communities, and societies. They have compiled legislation relevant to women's rights at the international and national levels, as well as in family law.

Center for Women's Global Leadership, Douglass College, Rutgers, The State University of New Jersey, 160 Ryders Lane, New Brunswick NJ 08901-8555, USA. Tel: +1 732 932 8782; Fax: +1 732 932 1180
cwgl@igc.org
www.cwgl.rutgers.edu

The Center for Women's Global Leadership (Global Center) develops women's leadership for women's human rights and social justice worldwide. Its programmes promote the leadership of women and advance feminist perspectives in policy-making processes in local, national, and international arenas. They focus on policy and advocacy, and leadership development and women's human rights.

Women's Environment and Development Organization (WEDO), 355 Lexington Avenue, 3rd Floor, New York, NY 10017-6603, USA. Tel: +1 212 973 0325; Fax: +1 212 973 0335
wedo@wedo.org
www.wedo.org

WEDO is an international advocacy network which promotes women's equality in decision making in governance and in policy-making institutions, forums, and processes, at all levels, to achieve economic and social justice. A core programme is The Gender and Governance Program, which seeks women's full and equal access to all areas and all levels of public life, working towards gender balance in terms of participation and representation, especially in government.

United Nations International Research and Training Institute for the Advancement of Women – Gender Awareness Information and Networking System (UN INSTRAW-GAINS), César Nicolás Penson 102-A, Santo Domingo, República Dominicana.
Tel: +1 809 685 2111; Fax: +1 809 685 2117
comments@un-instraw.org
www.un-instraw.org

Aiming to promote gender equality and women's advancement worldwide through research, training, and the collection and dissemination of information, INSTRAW was established in 1976. With the recent establishment of the Gender Awareness Information and Networking System, INSTRAW is now able to further gender equality and the empowerment of women through a user-driven virtual community and ICT-based learning tool for creating and sharing knowledge to improve development policy and practice.

The Centre for Research and Training on Development (CRTD), Achrafieh 11 00 2030 Beirut, Lebanon. Tel: +961 1 611079; Fax: +961 1 612924
info@crtd.org
www.crtd.org
www.macmag-glip.org
www.iris-Lebanon.org

CRTD is a forum for debate, learning, capacity building, training, and exchange on women, gender, and development among interested groups in the Middle East and Maghreb region. Identifying citizenship as a key thematic issue of importance to women throughout the Machreq/ Maghreb region, CRTD launched in 2001 an on-going campaign on 'Women's Right to Nationality', involving networking, capacity building, research, and lobbying components. Regional research on 'Arab Women's Right to Nationality and the Denial of Citizenship' was initiated in partnership with UNDP's Programme on Governance in the Arab Region, and with the support of IDRC.

Centre of Arab Women for Training and Research (CAWTAR), 44 Avenue de Pologne, 1005 El Omrane, Tunis, Tunisia. Tel: +216 71 571 945 / +216 71 571 867; Fax: +216 71 574 627
cawtar@planet.tn
www.cawtar.org.tn

The Center of Arab Women for Training and Research (CAWTAR) is an international non-government institution, established in 1993 and located in Tunisia. It aims to promote Arab women's participation in development by providing gender training, research, clearing-house services, and advisory services. The main programmes of CAWTAR are a periodical report (*Arab Women Development (AWD) Report*); training on gender issues and advocacy and media; and collection of gender-disaggregated information. CAWTAR has already published its first two AWD reports and is working on three forthcoming titles: 'Women and Decision-Making', 'Women and Legislation', and 'Women and Media'.

Association for the Enhancement and Development of Women, ADEW, 8/10 Mathaf al Manial Street, POB 1065 El Atab, Cairo, Egypt. Tel: +202 364 4324; Fax: +202 363 45
adew@link.net
www.adewegypt.org

ADEW is an Egyptian organisation working to improve the status of women through promoting legal and social empowerment, as well as providing credit and income-generating opportunities. ADEW is the first organisation in Egypt to assist low-income women to obtain identity cards and other legal documents. ADEW is involved in a study on the issuing of identity cards as a basic right of citizenship. The study is part of the UNDP POGAR gender and citizenship programme (see Electronic Resources section).

Note: Much of the literature and work being done on gender and citizenship has focused on the Middle East, a fact which is reflected in the predominance of the region in this resources section.